CW00369644

On Your Bike
around
Bristol and Bath

Nigel Vile

COUNTRYSIDE BOOKS
NEWBURY BERKSHIRE

First published 2001
© Nigel Vile 2001

All rights reserved.
No reproduction permitted without the prior
permission of the publisher:

COUNTRYSIDE BOOKS
3 Catherine Road
Newbury, Berkshire

ISBN 1 85306 660 5

Designed by Graham Whiteman

Photographs by the author
Maps by the author and
redrawn by Gelder design & mapping

Produced through MRM Associates Ltd., Reading
Printed in Singapore

CONTENTS

AREA MAP SHOWING THE LOCATIONS OF THE RIDES

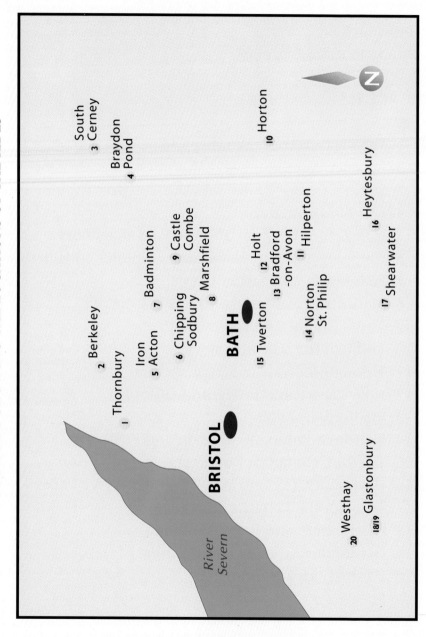

INTRODUCTION

C ycling is currently experiencing a phase of almost unrivalled popularity. Not only is this exhilarating pastime seen as being particularly healthy, it also corresponds with a time of increasing environmental awareness in society. Even city commuters are taking to the saddle in significant numbers, a fact not unconnected with the congestion that can reduce motorised journey times to almost walking pace in Britain's major conurbations. For most of the population, however, cycling is still a leisure activity, something to be enjoyed at weekends and in the holidays in the countryside.

The area around Bristol and Bath might at first sight not appear to be perfect cycling country. Whether one stands alongside the Royal Crescent in Bath or St Augustine's Parade in Bristol, the overriding image is one of hills. The magic and charm of both these West Country cities is their setting against a backdrop of the Cotswold Hills, the Mendip Hills and other lesser known upland areas. This is obviously not so magical for the cyclist, faced with the prospect of severe gradients and inclines on all sides! The reality, however, is far different. Within a short drive of both Bath and Bristol lie many locations that make for quite perfect cycling.

To the south-west lie the Somerset Levels, where the landscape has been described as 'excessively horizontal' by one guidebook writer. This is my own favourite spot for cycling, an area where the miles can be knocked off with the absolute minimum of effort. To the north lie both the Severn Vale and the Cotswold Plateau, where once again the gradients are gentle, and occasionally non-existent. Head east into Wiltshire, and localities such as the Vale of Pewsey and the Wylye Valley provide idyllic cycling opportunities. Of course, there is the occasional hill encountered on the majority of these circuits, but the general lack of significant inclines will surely come as a surprise to many would-be cyclists.

Added to the natural landscape, there are the villages, hamlets and historical sites along the way. Picture postcard villages, such as Lacock and Castle Combe; industrial heritage, such as the Kennet and Avon Canal; grand properties, such as Chalfield Manor and Longleat House; ancient towns, such as Bradford-on-Avon and Chipping Sodbury . . . all of this and so much more will be discovered on these routes. All that remains is for you to choose a route, hitch on the cycle rack to your vehicle and head off to one of these cycle tours that lie within close proximity to either Bath or Bristol. I wish you many hours of relaxing cycling in one of the most attractive corners of Britain.

Nigel Vile

GUIDE TO USING THIS BOOK

Each route is preceded by information to help you:

The **route title** tells you either the main places that you will start from or pass through, or the geographical locality in which the circuit is based. Because many cyclists will arrive at the starting point by car, each route ends where it begins. However, of course, it is possible to start and finish the route wherever you want.

The **number of miles** is the total for the ride. Most rides are along roads which, unlike some tracks, can be ridden at any time of the year. There are a small number of routes which contain sections of off-road cycling, chiefly sections of canal towpath. Although opposed by the majority of cyclists, it is still officially the case that towpath cyclists should have a permit, available from the British Waterways Board (telephone 01380 722859).

The brief **introduction** to the ride gives a broad picture of where the route goes and also mentions particular features that you will see.

The **starting point** names a village or town and gives its location in the Bath and Bristol area in relation to other towns/villages and to main roads. All the routes give a specific starting point within the town or village. Wherever possible, this will be a public car park.

Places for refreshment, sometimes a particular pub or tearoom,

are mentioned in the pre-ride information. There are also suggestions for picnic locations in some of the routes. Do not forget Paragraph 211 of the Highway Code: You MUST NOT ride under the influence of drink or drugs.

An indication is given of the **nature of the terrain** and the severity of any gradients that you will encounter, and of particularly busy main roads.

THE ROUTES

It is a good idea to read right through a route before setting out so that you note any places where you want to spend more time. The routes have been arranged according to their location in relation to Bath and Bristol, rather than to their length of difficulty, so just choose ones you like the look of.

Each route is set out in numbered sections, with each number corresponding with a location on the route map. The directions have been written as clearly as possible. Instructions to turn left or right are printed in bold, like this: **Turn L** at the T-junction. Instructions to continue straight over a crossroads or carry straight on are not in bold.

The directions may well include a brief comment on the route, but at the end of each circuit there is more information about **places of interest**.

The map of the area around Bath and Bristol on page 4 shows where the 20 routes are situated. A simple **sketch map** accompanies each route. These maps are intended to give you a general idea of where the routes go but are not detailed enough to be route guides. The relevant OS Landranger Series map is always recommended. This is particularly the case where a route follows a section of canal towpath, which may occasionally be closed for seasonal repairs.

SAFETY

Make sure that your bike and those of any companions – especially children – are roadworthy. This book is about routes not repairs, so seek elsewhere for do-it-yourself information or a good bike mechanic. It is unwise to set off knowing that, say, your gears are not working properly or your saddle is too low. Get things checked before you go, especially if you are riding an unfamiliar bike.

Decide in advance what you are going to do if your bike gets a puncture, and be prepared. There is no point in equipping yourself with a puncture outfit if you don't know how to use it. It might be better to take a spare inner tube – plus the tools you will need – but of course you will need to know how to deal with this, too. A mobile phone might be the best

insurance policy, assuming that there is someone to phone who is prepared to come and rescue you!

Make sure you don't have things dangling off handlebars or panniers.

Locking your bike will be completely unnecessary in most of the places where these routes take you but use your common sense and lock if in doubt. This is particularly the case when stopping at a pub for lunch.

Safe cycling

Wear comfortable clothes and shoes. Wear a helmet.

Stop if you want to consult a map or this book, otherwise you may ride into a car or a ditch.

If you are with someone else or a group make sure that the pace suits everyone, and arrange that those who are ahead will stop at intervals to give the others time to catch up and get their breath before setting off again. If you are one of the fastest don't forget that the people behind you may not be so fit, so practised or so fond of cycling as you are. Look after them.

If you find yourself cycling in traffic you may feel safer to walk and push your bike, even if you extend your journey by half an hour.

Riding after dark is dangerous even with lights. Be very careful if you do so.

Thornbury, Berkeley and Shepperdine

20 miles

Sandwiched between the Cotswold escarpment and the River Severn, the Vale of Berkeley stretches from Frampton-on-Severn in the north down to Thornbury, a commuter town a few miles north of Bristol. This is perfect cycling country, an almost horizontal landscape with just the occasional undulation to raise the heartbeat. The economy of the Vale of Berkeley is still dominated by small family-owned farms and this lends the area an old-fashioned feel, where the visitor may indeed feel that time has stood still. From Thornbury the route goes north along quiet roads to Berkeley. The town is perhaps best-known for being the birthplace of the smallpox pioneer Edward Jenner, although it is Berkeley Castle that attracts most visitors to this quiet backwater that lies alongside the Severn estuary. No byway or lane borders the riverbank, so it is necessary to make a brief detour at Shepperdine in order to visit this most impressive of England's rivers. The detour is well worthwhile, however, with a most welcoming hostelry lying immediately below the Severn's flood defences! The return route is through another picturesque settlement, at Oldbury on Severn.

Map: OS Landranger 162 Gloucester and the Forest of Dean (GR 633906).

Starting point: Thornbury church. From the A38, north of Bristol, take the B4061 into Thornbury. Once into this small town, follow the signs for Thornbury Castle that lies alongside the church. There is ample room for roadside parking near the church.

Refreshments: There are many opportunities for rest and refreshment along the way, with pubs in Thornbury, Ham, Berkeley, Shepperdine and Oldbury-on-Severn. My own personal favourite is the Windbound Inn on the Severn at Shepperdine. The name came from the bargees who once plied their trade along the river. Their excuse for delays was that they had been 'windbound', when the reality was a drinking session at what was then called the New Inn. The nickname for the inn clearly stuck, and has stood the passage of time!

The route: This circuit will be within the capabilities of just about every cyclist – indeed, it would make a suitable excursion for fairly active family groups.

---

1. Continue along Park Road from the church, passing the Castle School and Manor Brook School, before joining the B4061 in ½ mile. **Turn L**, and follow the B4061 for ½ mile to a junction just past Mile End Farm.

At this junction, **turn L** along the road

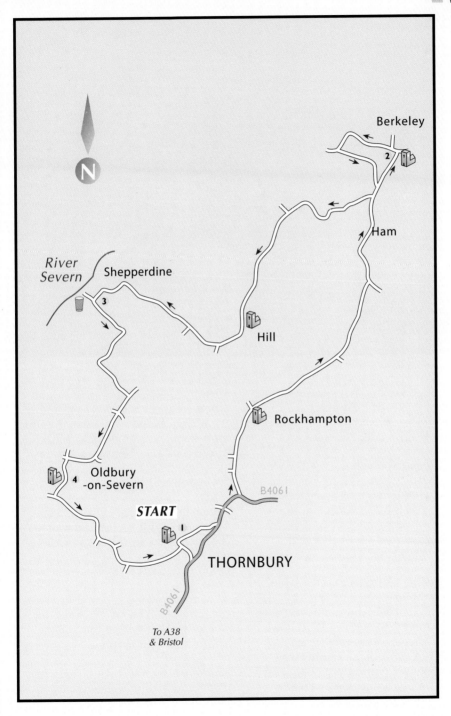

Berkeley

2

Ham

*River
Severn* Shepperdine

3

Hill

Rockhampton

Oldbury
-on-Severn 4

B4061

START

1

THORNBURY

B4061

*To A38
& Bristol*

Thornbury castle seen from the churchyard

signposted to Rockhampton and Hill. Follow this road for 4 miles, passing through Rockhampton whilst ignoring all side turns along the way.

Eventually, you will reach a T-junction immediately past a bridge over a small stream – the right turn is signposted to Stone and the A38. **Turn L** at this junction, along the lane to Berkeley. Follow the road for 2 miles into Berkeley's Market Place.

2. Turn L, and keep directly ahead along the road signposted to the Power Station, ignoring the 'main' road that bears right to Sharpness. Head down Salter Street out of Berkeley, passing both the Mariners Arms and Boars Head pubs. Continue out of Berkeley for ¾ mile to a junction just past a bridge over Berkeley Pill.

Turn L – there is no signpost – and follow what is Hamfield Lane back to the road in Ham by the Salutation Inn. **Turn R** and, at a junction in 150 yards just beyond Ham's village green, **turn R** along the lane signposted to Clapton, Bevington and Hill.

Follow this lane for 3 miles into Hill. Cycle out of Hill, and continue along the 'main' lane for 2½ miles to a T-junction on the edge of Shepperdine, ignoring two left turns along the way.

3. At this junction, a detour **to the R** – signposted to 'The River' – will bring you to the Windbound Inn and the Severn in just 100 yards.

For the main route, **turn L** along the road signposted to Shepperdine and Thornbury. Follow this road for 2 miles to its junction with the Hill to Oldbury road.

Turn R, and continue for 600 yards to a crossroads. Continue straight ahead towards Oldbury village. In ¾ mile, at a T-junction, **turn R** along the road signposted to Oldbury and Cowhill. In another 600 yards, at a junction by Oldbury's Methodist church, keep on the road that **bears L** to reach the Anchor Inn.

4. Continue uphill beyond the inn, passing the village school and St Arilda's church. Keep on the 'main' road that drops downhill into Cowhill.

Continue along this road for 2½ miles as it climbs gently back into Thornbury, ignoring all side turnings. The route

enters Thornbury via Kington Lane. At its junction with Castle Street, **turn L** to return to the church.

● ●

THORNBURY

Once best known as a market town, Thornbury is now very much a commuter base for people who work in Bristol. The town is heavily associated with Edward Stafford, Duke of Buckingham, who was beheaded during the reign of Henry VIII for treason. Stafford had begun work on Thornbury Castle and Henry, suspicious of his ambitions, summoned Stafford to London. He was subsequently executed on Tower Hill, whilst the castle at Thornbury was confiscated by the King. Henry VIII and Anne Boleyn actually stayed at the castle in 1533 rather than visiting Bristol, which at the time was

St Arilda's church

inflicted with the plague. Although very much a private property, parts of the castle can be seen from the church at the start of this circuit.

BERKELEY

A tranquil little town that sits near the Severn Estuary. Its fine castle, home to the Berkeley family for close on 800 years, rises above the Little Avon River and its water meadows. That this is a homely residence can be seen from the tall chimneys that rise above the battlements, as well as the mullioned windows that sit snugly in the castle walls. In 1327, Edward II was murdered in Berkeley Castle by his jailers, and the fortress was besieged by the Roundheads during the Civil War, an event that is marked by a huge breach in the wall of the castle's keep. Edward Jenner, who discovered the smallpox vaccine, was born in Berkeley in 1749, and his earthly remains lie in the local churchyard. The 18th century Chantry near the church was Jenner's home, and houses the fascinating Jenner Museum.

OLDBURY ON SEVERN

The settlement may not lie on the river itself, but the presence of this great waterway was certainly felt by villagers in centuries past, when floods frequently swamped the local low-lying land. To the south of the village lies St Arilda's church, elevated on a small hill or knoll, from where a fine view is obtained. Downstream lies the first Severn Bridge, whilst upstream can be seen the towers of Oldbury Power Station. Across the river are Chepstow, the Forest of Dean and the foothills of the Welsh Mountains. St Arilda, incidentally, makes an interesting study. Martyred at nearby Kington by a certain Muncius à Tiraunt, her crime was simply that she would not consent to 'lie' with him.

Edward Jenner's house

2

Berkeley, Slimbridge and Sharpness

19 miles

This circuit explores the northern part of the Vale of Berkeley, a relatively flat tract of land that lies between the Cotswold escarpment and the Severn estuary. The route follows quiet lanes and byways, as well as a section of canal towpath. Starting in Berkeley itself, you head northwards to Slimbridge, before following the Gloucester and Sharpness Canal through to the port of Sharpness. The settlements along the way could not provide more of a contrast. Stinchcombe sits on the Cotswold Edge, and is very much a Cotswold village, whilst Slimbridge is a scattered settlement of old and new dwellings, with its best known feature being the Wildfowl Trust. Sharpness may prove something of an acquired taste! This working port, where sea-going vessels once left the Severn to follow the canal network northwards to Gloucester and the Midlands, is quite simply not the type of place one associates with Gloucestershire. From Sharpness, it is just a mile-or-two of cycling back into Berkeley.

Map: OS Landranger 162 Gloucester and the Forest of Dean (GR 684993).

Starting point: The public car park near the Market Place in Berkeley. Follow the A38 northwards from Bristol to a turning just beyond Newport signposted to Berkeley and Sharpness. Follow the signs into Berkeley and, at the end of the Market Place, keep on the road which bears right towards Sharpness; 100 yards along this road, turn right into the car park that is just before the Bird in Hand Hotel.

Refreshments: A detour from the towpath at Purton will bring you to the Berkeley Arms Inn alongside the Severn Estuary. This hostelry is a personal favourite. On a clear sunny day, with views across the river towards the Forest of Dean, there can be fewer more pleasant spots to rest awhile and enjoy liquid refreshment.

The route: East of Berkeley, the busy A38 has to be crossed en route to Stinchcombe, whilst beyond Stinchcombe, a very short stretch of the same road has to be followed en route to Slimbridge. From Slimbridge through to Sharpness, the route follows the towpath of the Gloucester and Sharpness Canal. This is a grassy surface – rather than tarmac or gravel – and would be muddy following heavy rainfall. Plan your day out accordingly!

1. From Berkeley's Market Place follow the main road out of this small town towards the A38. In 600 yards, at a roundabout, continue ahead for 200

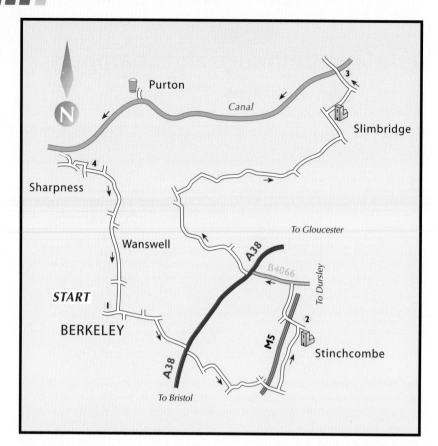

yards before taking an unsigned **R turn** by Mobley Farm.

Follow this occasionally busy unclassified road for ³/₄ mile to the A38. **Turn R and, in just 30 yards,** L along the lane signposted to Hogsdown, Lower and Upper Wick.

In ¹/₄ mile, take an unsigned **L turn** and follow what is a very minor lane for ³/₄ mile to a junction by a railway bridge. **Turn L,** and continue for ¹/₂ mile to a crossroads.

At this crossroads, **turn R** along the road signposted to North Nibley and

Stinchcombe. In 600 yards, having crossed the M5 motorway, **turn L** along the road signposted to Stinchcombe. Follow this road for 1³/₄ miles to a road junction in Stinchcombe by the church.

2. **Turn L** – signposted to Berkeley Road and Gloucester – and follow Echo Lane for ³/₄ mile down to its junction with the B4066. **Turn L,** and follow the B4066 for ¹/₂ mile to the A38.

Turn L, pass the Prince of Wales Hotel, cross a railway line and then **turn R** along the road signposted to Breadstone, Halmore and Purton. Follow this road for 1³/₄ miles as far as a

The Gloucester and Sharpness Canal

sharp left-hand bend. On this bend, **turn R** – there is no signpost – to enter the diminutive hamlet of Halmore.

In 100 yards, **turn R** into Slimbridge Lane – signposted to Gossington and Slimbridge. In 2¼ miles, **turn L** into Moorend Lane – signposted to Slimbridge. Follow this lane for ¾ mile to its junction with St Johns Road in Slimbridge. **Turn L** – signposted to the Wildfowl Trust – and cycle through Slimbridge passing the church.

In ½ mile, on the edge of the village, **turn R** by Hurns Farm along the lane signposted to Troytown. Follow this lane for ½ mile to a junction by Hope House Farm. **Turn L**, and follow a cul-de-sac lane for ½ mile down to the Gloucester and Sharpness Canal.

3. Cross the canal, and follow the towpath **to the L** for ¾ mile to a road – this section of the towpath is a proper cyclepath. Cross the road, and continue following the towpath for 2½ miles into Purton. In Purton, two consecutive bridges cross the canal. A detour to the right at the second of these bridges will bring you to the Berkeley Arms Inn.

For the main route, continue following the towpath beyond the second of these bridges – initially it is signposted as a 'Private Road'. Follow the towpath for 1¾ miles to Sharpness Marina.

At the end of the marina, push your cycle across a pontoon **on the left** and follow some steps and a footpath uphill to the marina car park. Follow

15

the road up and out of the parking area, before **bearing R** by a wooden bungalow to drop downhill towards the dock complex.

On reaching a junction by some warehouses, **turn L and immediately L again** to follow a road across a series of bridges. Beyond the final brick bridge, **bear R** in front of the Severn View Nursing Home.

4. In just a few yards, **turn L** along the road signposted to Brookend and Purton. At a junction in ¼ mile, **turn R** along the road to Brookend and Berkeley. Pass through Brookend, passing the Lammastide Inn, to reach a junction.

Turn L – signposted to Berkeley – pass the Salmon Inn at Wanswell and continue for 1 mile to a roundabout. Continue straight ahead into Berkeley, and in ¼ mile you will reach the car park on the left-hand side.

The signpost in Stinchcombe village

BERKELEY

See the notes with the previous ride.

PURTON

The New Grounds north of Purton, hundreds of acres of mud flats bordering the Severn, are part of the Slimbridge Wildfowl Trust, established in 1946 by the late Sir Peter Scott. Signs opposite the Berkeley Arms Inn emphasise the importance of the New Grounds for wildfowl, public access being strictly limited. The reason for this is quite simple – this is the wintering ground for 5,000 white-fronted geese, over half of the British population of this Russian-breeding species. The New Grounds are also winter home for up to 400 Bewick's swans, 5% of the European population.

THE GLOUCESTER AND SHARPNESS CANAL

The canal was constructed in the early 19th century to bypass the shallow meandering waters of the upper reaches of the Severn Estuary. Built as a ship canal able to accommodate vessels of up to 800 tons, it effectively made Gloucester a major inland port. The grand dimensions of this 16 mile long canal, particularly its 90 foot width, made it second only to the Manchester Ship Canal in terms of importance and tonnage handled. At Purton, two swing-bridges cross the canal, and the village boasts a typical example of a bridge-keeper's house complete with stucco and painted Doric columns, an architectural feature that was fashionable in the early 19th century.

16

The Berkeley Arms, Purton

SHARPNESS DOCKS

Sharpness Docks were constructed where the Gloucester and Sharpness Canal joined the River Severn. The Old Dock, consisting of a small basin, a lock house and the original entrance lock from the Severn, was constructed in 1827. Within 40 years, the basin was so congested that a new larger dock was essential. The New Dock was opened in 1874 and is able to accommodate ocean-going vessels of up to 5,000 tons. This was essentially a greenfield site for the port, and the Sharpness New Dock Company therefore had to construct a complete dock village, including shipping offices, terraced housing for the dock workers and a school for their children. Today, the docks are thriving, with new warehouse development continuing apace, whilst the approach to the Old Dock is a thriving marina.

3

South Cerney, Kemble and the Cotswold Water Park

21 miles

This is a gentle, undemanding ride, which explores the countryside in and around the Cotswold Water Park. Located a few miles south of Cirencester, the Water Park is a collection of lakes that have resulted from gravel extraction in the Upper Thames Valley. Starting from South Cerney, a picturesque village full of Cotswold charm, the circuit passes through a number of other villages on the Cotswold fringe before reaching Kemble, best known for being the nearest settlement to the source of the Thames. From Kemble, the route returns eastwards back to South Cerney by way of Ewen and Siddington, crossing Old Father Thames along the way. Given the generally flat nature of the terrain, you will have ample time and energy to explore and savour the various villages along the way.

Map: OS Landranger 163 Cheltenham and Cirencester (GR 062968).

Starting point: The Lakeside car park near South Cerney. From Crudwell, on the A429 from Malmesbury to Cirencester, follow the unclassified road that heads eastwards to Oaksey. This becomes the Water Park Spine Road. In 9 miles, shortly before its junction with the A419, turn left at a crossroads along the road signposted to South Cerney – this is Station Road. The car park lies a short distance along this turning.

Refreshments: There are pubs in South Cerney, Cerney Wick, Ashton Keynes, Kemble, Ewen and Siddington, giving you ample choice along the route. The Wild Duck at Ewen in particular comes highly recommended, a hostelry that seldom fails to appear in the pages of the *Good Pub Guide*. Another alternative is to take a picnic, which can be enjoyed alongside the lake by the car park at journey's end.

The route: Although the roads are unclassified, you may find more vehicles than you would expect hereabouts due to the number of visitors who flock to the Cotswold Water Park.

1. Return to Station Road, **turn L** and cycle down to the Spine Road. Cross over and follow the lane opposite signposted to Cerney Wick. Follow this lane for 2¼ miles, passing through Cerney Wick, before continuing to a road junction.

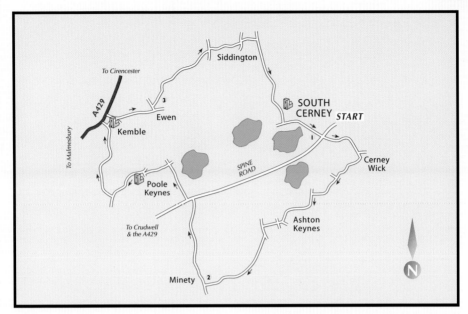

Turn **L** at this junction – there is no sign – passing the entrance to a quarry, and continue on to Ashton Keynes. At a T-junction just past some new houses, **turn R** and cycle along to a crossroads.

Head straight over – signposted to Minety – initially crossing a stream before continuing for ¼ mile to the next junction. **Turn L** and, in 200 yards, having crossed Swill Brook, **turn R** along the lane leading to Minety. Follow this lane for 1¾ miles to a junction on the fringes of Minety.

2. Turn R – signposted to Somerford Keynes – and follow this road for 2 miles to the Spine Road. **Turn L** and, in 200 yards, **turn R** along the lane to Old Manor Farm. In ¾ mile, at a minor crossroads, **turn L** past a bungalow.

In ½ mile, at a junction in Poole Keynes, **turn R** and cycle up to the next junction by the village cross.

Turn **L** – signposted to Oaksey – and head out of the village, passing the church along the way.

In ½ mile, **turn R** at a junction along the lane to Kemble. On reaching the church and war memorial in Kemble, **turn R** down Church Road to the next junction. **Turn R**, and cycle for 1 mile through to Ewen, crossing the infant Thames along the way.

3. In Ewen, **turn L** along the road signposted to Siddington and Coates. In just 100 yards, **keep R** at a fork, still following the road to Siddington.

Follow this road for 1½ miles to a T-junction. **Turn L** and, in 75 yards, **turn R** along the road to Siddington. Follow this road for ½ mile, passing a recreation ground, to a junction by the local store in Siddington.

Turn L, passing some red-brick cottages, before **turning R** along the

19

A tranquil spot in the Cotswold Water Park

road to Preston and South Cerney. In $^1/_4$ mile, at the next junction, **turn R** and cycle the 2 miles through to South Cerney.

At the end of the main street known as Clarks Hay, by the War Memorial, **turn L** along the road to Cricklade and Cerney Wick. The car park is on the left-hand side in just $^1/_2$ mile.

● ● ● ● ● ● ● ● ● ● ● ● ● ● ● ● ● ● ● ●

THE COTSWOLD WATER PARK

The Cotswold Water Park can boast as many as 75 lakes in a diminutive swathe of countryside stretching from Kemble to Cricklade. The lakes, the result of gravel extraction in the Upper Thames Valley, now provide one of the region's fastest growing leisure facilities, with activities as diverse as bird-watching and sailing,

fishing and jet-skiing being available for visitors. For ornithologists, this is one of the more important sites in Southern Britain, with over 200 bird species having been recorded. The species that live in- and-around the lakes all year round include grebes, heron, pochard, dippers and Canada geese, whilst in the winter months, roosting gulls in their thousands abound in the area.

SOUTH CERNEY

A picturesque Cotswold village on the banks of the River Churn, it is now more than 60 years since Arthur Mee, in his *King's England* guide to Gloucestershire penned an eloquent description of South Cerney. He wrote: 'Here flows the Churn, tributary of the Thames, singing its quiet way past cottage doors and giving its name to the village – Churney. Very

Time for a rest!

beautiful is the village with its stream, its thatched and tiled cottages with their dormer windows, its houses of Cotswold stone, and its noble church with much treasure from far-off days.' Even allowing for poetic licence, this description in no way exaggerates the beauty of this fine settlement.

KEMBLE

Kemble grew in importance when it became an important railway junction during the 19th century. Travellers would alight at the local station to join the branch lines south to Tetbury and north to Cirencester. Sadly, only the main line through the village from Swindon to Gloucester remains, but there is still much in Kemble to detain the interested visitor. The line of the old Thames and Severn Canal passes to the north of the village, where intrepid explorers will also find the source of Old Father Thames. There is also the church, largely rebuilt in the 19th century, whose south transept was brought from nearby Ewen where it had served as a chapel. There is a fine Norman inner doorway, as well as an effigy of a 13th-century knight in chain mail, hidden away behind the organ.

21

4
East of Malmesbury
20 miles

This is a pleasant cycle ride through an undulating slice of the North Wiltshire countryside. Along the way lie a number of villages, including Great and Little Somerford with their decidedly Cotswold feel. This was once the heart of a vast area of woodland known as Braydon Forest, a remnant of which remains at Somerford Common. Other natural features along the way include Braydon Pond, on the fringes of Braydon Wood, and the upper reaches of the River Avon as it heads south towards Chippenham and Bath.

The churches at Great and Little Somerford are included in John Betjeman's *Parish Churches*. Betjeman was of the opinion that it was 'worth bicycling twelve miles against the wind' to visit these fine ecclesiastical buildings. I sincerely hope that you do not have to suffer the experience of this much-quoted phrase when using this book!

Map: OS Landranger 173 Swindon and Devizes (GR 999883).

Starting point: The roadside by Braydon Pond. Follow the B4044 east from Malmesbury towards Minety and 5 miles from Malmesbury, head south along a side turning signposted to Garston and Brinkworth. In ¾ mile, park on the roadside by Braydon Pond.

Refreshments: There are pubs along the way at both Minety and Brinkworth, although it is worth persevering as far as Great Somerford, 5 miles from the end of the ride, to enjoy refreshment at the ever-popular Volunteer Inn.

The route: Although the route crosses a relatively gentle landscape, there are occasional inclines along the way that will set the pulses racing. The climb up into Brinkworth has its rewards in a long downhill stretch below Callow Hill, whilst sections of the ride from Little Somerford back to Braydon Pond will put those leg muscles to the test.

---

1. Cycle back up to the B4040 and **turn R**, signposted to Minety and Cricklade. In ¾ mile, **turn L** along Dog Trap Lane, signposted to Minety Church and Oaksey. In another ¾ mile, at a T-junction, **turn R** along the road signposted to Cricklade.

Follow this road for ½ mile into Minety,

before continuing along the main road through the village as it bears right to continue down to Minety crossroads, the B4040 and the Turnpike public house.

Head directly over at the crossroads, signposted to Braydon, Brinkworth and Wootton Bassett. Continue along this road for 600 yards before **turning R**

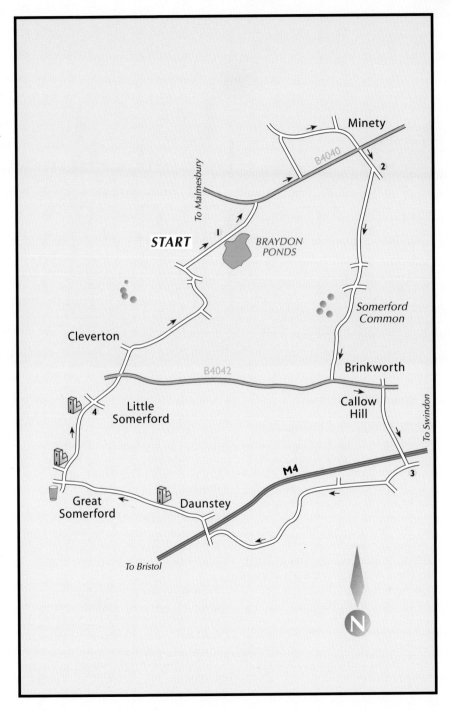

Minety

B4040

2

To Malmesbury

START   I   BRAYDON PONDS

Somerford Common

Cleverton

B4042

Brinkworth

Callow Hill

Little Somerford

4

To Swindon

M4

3

Great Somerford   Daunstey

To Bristol

N

Braydon Pond

along the road to Brinkworth.

2. Follow this lane for 1¾ miles to a crossroads. Continue directly ahead, still signposted to Brinkworth. In 300 yards, at a staggered crossroads, **turn R and then L** to enter the Forestry Commission's Somerford Common.

Follow the lane through the woodland and on for another 1¼ miles to reach the B4042 in Brinkworth. **Turn L**, and follow the B4042 past the Suffolk Arms and on for another ¾ mile to a crossroads in Callow Hill.

Turn R, signposted to Grittenham and Tockenham, and follow a lane downhill for 1¼ miles to a junction just beyond the M4 motorway.

3. Turn R along the road signposted to Dauntsey and Chippenham, and follow this road for 3½ miles, ignoring all side turns. The road eventually enters Dauntsey, and climbs up to a junction immediately to the south of the M4 motorway.

Turn R, signposted to Great Somerford and Brinkworth, and follow the road for 2 miles to a crossroads in Great Somerford by the Volunteer Inn.

Turn R, signposted to Little Somerford, and follow the road through the village up to the War Memorial. Keep on this road as it bears right, before passing the church. Continue for another 1 mile to a junction in neighbouring Little Somerford.

The route through Braydon Wood

R along the road signposted to Minety and Leigh. In just ½ mile, this lane reaches Braydon Pond.

●●●●●●●●●●●●●●●●●●●●●●●●●

BRAYDON FOREST

Braydon Forest was once part of a much larger area of woodland that stretched from the Thames Valley to Dorset, which was first mentioned in a charter of AD 796. This route explores a vestige of this former wooded corner of Wiltshire at Somerford Common, as well as passing the fringes of Braydon Wood. Set in the heart of Braydon Wood is Braydon Pond, which was the largest area of fresh water in North Wiltshire until nearby gravel workings at the Cotswold Water Park were flooded for recreational use. Braydon Pond provides a haven for grebe, heron, mallard, mute swan and tufted duck.

LITTLE AND GREAT SOMERFORD

These neighbouring villages are separated by just half-a-mile of meadow that borders the River Avon, the name *Somerford* originating in a former seasonal crossing point through the river. St Peter and St Paul's church in Great Somerford has a magnificent window in its south chancel that depicts Christ with six children of different races beneath two long-tailed Chinese dragons and a mosaic of towers and domes. The window is dedicated to the memory of the Reverend Lutley, Vicar of Somerford between 1952 and 1966, who served as a missionary in China from 1930 to 1944. Little Somerford's riposte is a Coat of Arms of Elizabeth I above the chancel screen, painted in 1602 as a reminder that the sovereign was head of the Church.

4. Turn L and then immediately R into Clay Street. Continue uphill for ¾ mile to the B4042. **Turn R** and, in 100 yards, **turn L** along the lane to Cleverton and Minety. Follow this lane down through Cleverton, ignoring a left turn to Leigh. Continue along this lane for another 1¼ miles as it climbs away from Cleverton to reach a junction.

Turn L, signposted to Charlton and Purton, and continue for ½ mile to a T-junction immediately past Finch House. **Turn L** – signposted to Charlton.

In just ¼ mile, by Little Elm Farm, **turn**

5

Iron Acton, Wickwar and the Vale of Sodbury

24 miles

Acursory glance at the Ordnance Survey map would suggest that the area north of Iron Acton on the fringes of the former Bristol Coalfield, might pose some problems for cyclists – the area simply looks too developed! The reality is very different, however. The roads and byways are surprisingly devoid of traffic, the locality is pleasantly rural and the slight elevations along the way bring many a pleasing vista across the South Gloucestershire countryside. There are even one or two surprises on the route, none more so than the commons at Hawkesbury and Inglestone, whilst the outlook towards the Cotswold escarpment above Hawkesbury is especially fine.

Map: OS Landranger 172 Bristol and Bath (GR 680836).

Starting point: The High Street in Iron Acton near the church. Iron Acton lies just off the B4058 that runs from Bristol to Yate, and the village centre is clearly signposted. The High Street is the main street in the village, running from the White Hart Inn through to the church. Park on the roadside in the High Street.

Refreshments: There are pubs along the way at Wickwar and Tytherington, whilst at journey's end, Iron Acton can offer both the White Hart and the Swan Inn. The Swan Inn at Tytherington is perhaps an ideal option, lying just a few miles from journey's end. This is a large, well-furnished hostelry, that is welcoming to family groups. If your preference is a picnic, Inglestone Common between Orange End and Wickwar is as good a place as any to rest awhile.

The route: Although this is a generally level circuit, there are one or two hills along the way that will certainly raise the heartbeat. There is one climb up to the B4060 on the approach to Horton, a climb equalled as the route makes its way into Wickwar. Fortunately, these ascents are of relatively short duration. The roads and byways are generally quiet, although the busy B4058 has to be crossed at Iron Acton, whilst the short stretches of 'B' road followed near Wickwar and Latteridge can be busy at peak times.

---

1. Continue along the High Street as it bears left past the church to pass the Swan Inn, before reaching the traffic lights at the junction of the B4058 and B4059 roads. Cross the main road, and follow the B4058 opposite signposted to Wotton-under-Edge.

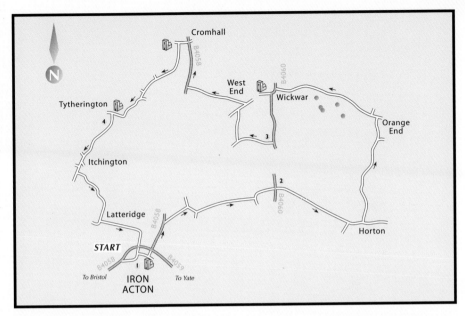

In ¾ mile, **turn R** into Chaingate Lane – there is no sign – and follow this road for ½ mile to a T-junction, ignoring a right turn called Dyers Lane along the way. **Turn R** at this junction and head down Manor Road for 250 yards and, where the road bears right, **turn L** into Tanhouse Lane, signposted to Yate Rocks and Wickwar.

Follow this lane for 1½ miles to a junction, and **keep L** along the 'main' lane signposted to Wickwar. Follow this lane up Bury Hill and onto the B4060 which is reached in just ½ mile.

2. Cross the B4060 and follow Mapleridge Lane opposite for 1¾ miles to a junction. **Turn L** at this junction and drop downhill into Horton.

In the middle of the village, opposite the Social Club, **turn L** into King Lane, signposted to Hawkesbury. Follow this lane for 1 mile to a cattle grid near Lower Chalkley Farm, before crossing Hawkesbury Common to reach a T-junction in the hamlet of Orange End, ignoring one right turn to Hawkesbury along the way.

Turn L – signposted to Wickwar – and continue to the B4060 in Wickwar, which is reached in 3 miles.

Turn L, and follow the B4060 signposted to Yate and Chipping Sodbury. Past the traffic lights that control traffic flows through a narrow part of the village, continue up into Wickwar's High Street before continuing south along the B4060 out of the village.

3. Just beyond the southern edge of Wickwar, **turn R** into Frith Lane – signposted to Hall End and Rangeworthy. In ¾ mile, **turn R** at a minor junction by a bungalow called Elm Croft. Follow this lane northwards for ¾ mile to a T-junction in West End, ignoring a left turn along the way.

Wickwar church with its handsome tower

Turn L – signposted to Cromhall – and follow the road ahead for 1½ miles to the B4058. **Turn R**, and follow the B4058 for 1 mile to a crossroads on the edge of Cromhall, before **turning L** along the lane signposted to St Andrew's church and the school.

Bear L in front of the school, and continue down Rectory Lane. Follow this lane for 1½ miles to a T-junction, ignoring two right turns en route. **Turn R**, and follow the road signposted to Thornbury into Tytherington, which is just ¾ mile away.

4. **Turn L** just past the Swan Inn along the lane to Itchington. Pass through the hamlet of Itchington in 1¼ miles – it is little more than a collection of farms – and continue along the main

lane for 600 yards to a **L turn** by Emlett Farm signposted to Latteridge and Iron Acton.

Follow this road – Latteridge Lane – for 1½ miles to the B4059 in Latteridge. **Turn L**, and follow this occasionally busy road down to the B4058 on the edge of Iron Acton. Cross over and follow the road opposite into the village, the village green is on the left. **Turn L** by the White Hart back into the High Street.

● ●

IRON ACTON
Iron Acton literally translates as 'the oak settlement with iron mines', although the Romans were in all probability the first and the last to extract iron locally. The church contains many memorials to the

one-time rulers of the locality, the Poyntz family. The family were related to the Tudors, and entertained such illustrious people as Elizabeth I and Sir Francis Drake at Acton Court. The 15th-century churchyard cross is a memorial to one member of the family, whilst the Poyntz Chapel within the church contains the helmet and a spur that were carried on the coffin of Sir John Poyntz, the last lord of the manor, who died in 1680.

WICKWAR

Wickwar was at one time a prosperous clothing town with its own mayor and corporation. This period in the town's history ran from the reign of Edward II through to the late 19th century. The main street in the town contains a number of handsome buildings, none more so than the Town Hall. Dating from the end of the 18th century, this centre of local government comes complete with bellcote and arches. One interesting fact relates to the Town Hall clock. Its mechanism, which dates from 1660, is believed to be the only one in the world with an escapement of 90 teeth! Hidden away at the end of a quiet cul-de-sac is the church, largely a 19th-century rebuilding. The guidebooks are quick to point out the Perpendicular west tower as well as a late 15th-century sculpture of St John the Baptist.

TYTHERINGTON

Best known for being a centre of quarrying activity, although the vast holes in the ground do not impinge upon this particular circuit. St James' church in the

May Day celebrations in Iron Acton

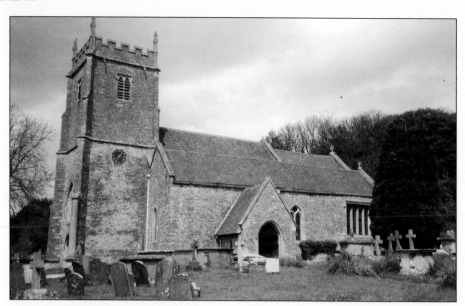

Tytherington church and its one-handed clock!

village, which dates from the 13th century, is noted for its curious one-handed clock. Opposite the church stands the Swan Inn, an ancient hostelry that, according to records kept by an earlier landlord, was selling ales to local residents as far back as 1608. Many fine 17th and 18th-century buildings can be seen in the village, including the 17th-century Grange near the church.

6

Chipping Sodbury, Hawkesbury Upton and Hillesley

16 miles

The local guidebooks describe the villages on this circuit as lying on the 'Cotswold Fringe', the countryside that straddles the border between the Severn Vale and the Cotswold landscape itself. In some senses, this does the area an injustice. Cycling down through the Kilcott Valley between Starveall and Hillesley, the rolling hillsides, stone cottages and clear streams could place the visitor anywhere in the heart of Cotswold country.

This fine excursion sets off from Chipping Sodbury, whose wide main street points to its former status as a market town, before reaching a short steep climb up the Cotswold escarpment at Little Sodbury. The route then crosses the open Cotswold plateau to reach Hawkesbury Upton, before dropping through the Kilcott Valley to Hillesley. Undulating countryside at the foot of the Cotswold escarpment is then crossed to reach Sodbury Common, Chipping Sodbury and journey's end. Quite simply, this is a delightful introduction for any visitor not familiar with the Southwolds.

Map: OS Landranger 172 Bristol and Bath (GR 728823).

Starting point: Broad Street, the main thoroughfare in Chipping Sodbury, where there is ample room for roadside parking.

Refreshments: Along the way, there are pubs at both Hawkesbury Upton and Hillesley, whilst at journey's end in Chipping Sodbury, you can take your choice from over a dozen inns, tea-rooms and restaurants. If your preference is for a picnic, both Hawkesbury Common and Sodbury Common are crossed along the way, both of which offer any number of delightful picnic opportunities.

The route: Apart from the relatively busy roads in the immediate vicinity of Chipping Sodbury, this route follows quiet lanes and byways through the South Gloucestershire countryside. There is one short, steep climb out of Little Sodbury onto the Cotswold Plateau, but this is more than compensated for by the long descent into the Kilcott Valley below Starveall.

---

1. Make for the east end of Broad Street, **turn L** by the War Memorial and follow Hatters Lane through an industrial estate to reach the Chipping Sodbury ring road. **Turn R and, in 30 yards**, L along the turning to Little Sodbury, Horton and Hawkesbury.

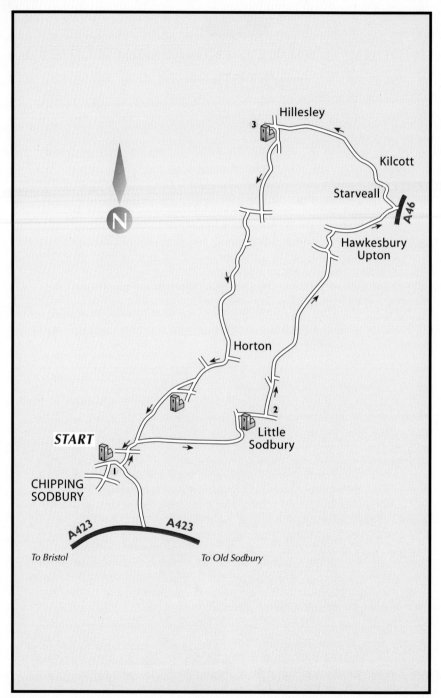

The rolling countryside near Hawkesbury Upton

Follow this lane for 2½ miles to a road junction in Hawkesbury Upton, **turn L** to the green and war memorial and then **turn R** along the lane to Starveall.

Follow this lane as it winds its way out of the village to reach a T-junction in ¼ mile. **Turn R**, and follow the lane that runs above the Kilcott Valley for 1 mile.

Just before the A46, **turn L** past a barn to follow a lane to Kilcott. Cross the hilltop, before dropping downhill into Kilcott, and then follow the lane through the valley to reach a road junction in Hillesley in 2½ miles.

3. Turn L past the Fleece Inn and the church and, on the edge of the village, **turn R** into Hawkesbury Road. Follow this lane for 1¼ miles to reach an isolated crossroads, **turn R** – signposted to Wickwar and Inglestone Common – and drop downhill to a cattle grid and the hamlet of Orange End. **Turn L**, signposted to Hawkesbury and Horton, and follow the lane for 2½ miles to Horton, crossing Hawkesbury Common along the way. At the junction by Horton Social Club, **turn R** towards Little Sodbury and Chipping Sodbury. In ½ mile, at the top of a climb in Totteroak, **fork L** into Little Sodbury End just past a bus shelter.

Drop downhill to a crossroads, and **turn R** across a cattle grid by Tyndale Baptist church onto Sodbury Common. In 600 yards, **turn L** at the next junction towards Chipping Sodbury.

Cross the Common to rejoin the ring road in 1 mile. **Turn R, then L** into Hatters Lane. Follow this lane back into Chipping Sodbury town centre.

Cross a cattle grid onto Sodbury Common, and almost straightaway **fork R** onto the lane to Little Sodbury. Follow this lane for 2 miles as it winds and climbs its way to Little Sodbury.

At the junction by Little Sodbury church, **turn R** along the road signposted to Horton and the A46. Head uphill for ½ mile – a very steep climb – to a junction on the hilltop. **Turn L** along the lane signposted to Horton and Hawkesbury.

2. Cross the hilltop for ½ mile until you join the road coming up from Horton to the A46. **Turn R** along this road and, in a short distance, where the 'main' road bears right to the A46, keep ahead along the side lane to Hawkesbury Upton.

CHIPPING SODBURY

Chipping Sodbury was first established in the 12th century by William le Gros, Lord of the Manor of Sodbury. In 1218, Henry III granted William's grandson a charter for a market and fairs, and the grid system street plan was laid out, with its wide market street and the long burgage plots behind its houses. The main street is full of fine old buildings that date back as far as the 16th century, stretching from the gabled 16th-century Grapes Hotel at the western end of the main street to the Portcullis, a 17th-century coaching inn that was once a meeting place for the Beaufort Hunt. In between are any number of old hostelries, with many archways, further reminders of the importance of Chipping Sodbury in the days of horse transport. The town was an important cloth centre until the 18th century, when the local cloth trade steadily declined. Being in a rich agricultural area, however, the town continued to thrive as a market centre, although today Chipping Sodbury is largely a base for commuting to Bristol.

HAWKESBURY UPTON

A hilltop village, located above the Cotswold Edge overlooking the Severn Vale. At one time, a market serving the local farming community existed in the village. The village could then boast no fewer than seven pubs, where the local farmers would gather each week to share a communal loaf, cheese and ale. A number of these pubs were celebrated in

Sodbury Common

Hillesley and its village cross

a local rhyme:

*'White Horse shall hunt Fox and drink the
Beaufort dry,
Turn the Barley Mow upside down and
make the Blue Boy cry.'*

Today, only the Fox and the Beaufort Inn
survive, and city commuters have largely
replaced the village's farming community.

HILLESLEY

Hillesley 'is not a Cotswold show village'
according to one local author. Rather 'it
has the atmosphere of a working village
with some very large and sometimes ugly
farm buildings and certain modern

development.' The original wealth and
prosperity of the village is explained in
the name of the local pub – the Fleece.
This is a reminder of the days when the
Cotswolds were a great wool producing
area. The neighbouring Kilcott Valley
once provided water-power for cloth
manufacturing, whilst in 1830 one
villager – George Oldland – patented a
rotary machine for shearing cloth.
Hillesley church dates from 1851, and is
based upon the designs of the Reverend
Benjamin Perkins. During this period of
large scale church restoration, many a
clergyman turned his hand to amateur
architecture – and many a critic would
say that it shows!

7

Badminton and Easton Grey

21 miles

Great Badminton is best known for being the venue for the annual three-day event that attracts horse enthusiasts from Britain, Europe and beyond. It is also the starting point for this delightful cycle ride that explores the landscape and villages of the Southern Cotswolds. With no fewer than ten picturesque Cotswold settlements along the way, with a rich variety of churches, grand houses and inns, this excursion is never short of interest.

From the Badminton Estate, the route heads northwards to cross the gently undulating countryside that lies between Didmarton and Shipton Moyne. It is then downhill into the Avon Valley, whose waters are crossed at the exquisite village of Easton Grey, before the circuit heads back across country to the fringes of Badminton Park and the village of Great Badminton itself.

Map: OS Landranger 173 Swindon and Devizes covers all but ½ mile of the route. The rogue ½ mile creeps onto OS Landranger 172 Bristol and Bath (GR 805825).

Starting point: The car park outside the Memorial Hall in Great Badminton. Make for the eastern end of Great Badminton's High Street, and just before the entrance to Badminton House, turn right into Hayes Lane. The Memorial Hall lies 150 yards along Hayes Lane.

Refreshments: Although Badminton itself has no public refreshment facilities – there is the Badminton Club for estate workers – there are pubs along the way at Didmarton and Leighterton. In all probability, however, you will stop off at Shipton Moyne. As well as being the halfway point on this circuit, who could resist an inn called 'The Cat and Custard Pot'?

The route: This is a relatively easy cycle ride through the gently undulating countryside of the Southwolds. There are occasional hills along the way, but these are either pretty short or capable of being cycled up without too much effort. Throughout, the roads and lanes are quiet and ideal for cyclists with relatively little traffic.

---

1. Return to the High Street in Great Badminton, **turn L** and, at a junction in just 100 yards, **turn R** to follow the main road out of the village.

Continue along this road for 1 mile to

Little Badminton and, 300 yards out of the village, **turn R** through a gateway opposite Shepherds Lodge.

Follow the estate road ahead, which shortly bears left to continue through

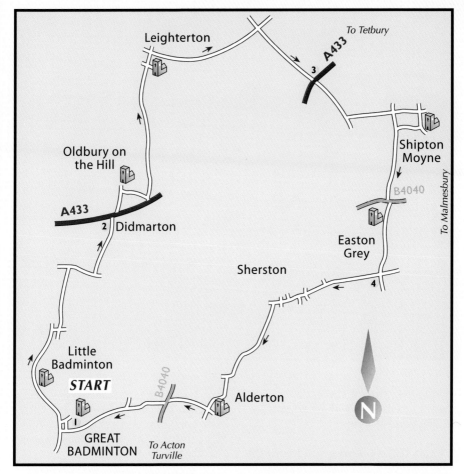

Badminton Great Park. Continue along this road for ¾ mile to a junction, before **turning R** to follow a road through Bullpark Wood. In 600 yards, at a junction just before a pair of cottages, **turn L** to follow a lane for 1 mile to the A433 on the edge of Didmarton.

2. Cross the A433 and follow the unsigned lane opposite towards Oldbury-on-the-Hill. In ½ mile, on entering this hamlet, **turn R**.

Follow the lane past farm buildings and on downhill for ½ mile to a road junction just before the A433. **Turn L** – signposted to Leighterton – and head north for 2 miles to reach this village.

Cycle through Leighterton, passing a pond, the church and the Royal Oak Inn, before reaching a crossroads in the heart of the village. **Turn R** – signposted Westonbirt and Tetbury – and follow the road out of the village, passing a cemetery on the left containing a number of war graves.

Continue along the road for 2 miles to

Oldbury-on-the-Hill

a crossroads, **turn R** and cycle for 1¼ miles up to the A433 in Westonbirt by the Hare and Hounds.

3. Cross the main road, and follow the road opposite signposted to Shipton Moyne and Easton Grey. In ¾ mile, **turn L** along the Shipton Moyne turning. Follow this lane for 1¼ miles to a crossroads on the edge of Shipton Moyne village. **Turn R**, and cycle through Shipton Moyne, passing the Cat and Custard Pot along the way.

At the southern end of the village, **bear R** off the main road to follow the turning signposted to Easton Grey. In ½ mile, at a T-junction, **turn L** along the road signposted to Easton Grey.

In 1¼ miles, on reaching the B4040,

turn L then R at a staggered crossroads to follow the lane down into the village of Easton Grey. Cross the River Avon, and continue out of the village to reach a crossroads in 1 mile.

4. Turn R – signposted to Luckington and Sherston. In 1¼ miles, keep straight on at a crossroads. In another 100 yards, **turn R** at a junction along the road signposted to Luckington and Sherston.

In another 100 yards, where the Sherston road bears right, keep ahead along an unsigned side lane. Continue along this lane for ¼ mile to the second crossroads, and **turn L** along the road signposted to Alderton and Grittleton.

In 1½ miles, **turn L** at the next junction along the road signposted to Alderton. In just ¼ mile, **turn R** and cycle into Alderton itself. Follow the road through the village to a crossroads by a pond, and **turn R** along the Badminton turning.

In ½ mile, on reaching the B4040, **turn L** in the direction of Acton Turville and Badminton. In just 200 yards, **turn R** off the B4040 onto the lane signposted to Badminton.

Follow this lane for 1¾ miles back into Great Badminton, where the **first turning on the R** is Hayes Lane. Cycle down this lane for 150 yards back to the Memorial Hall.

GREAT BADMINTON

Great Badminton is chiefly an estate village, centred on the wide High Street that leads to Badminton House, the ancestral home of the Duke of Beaufort. The attractive row of almshouses, dating from the early 18th century, comes complete with the Beaufort portcullis and the Beaufort beasts supporting the cartouches. Badminton House itself is a strictly private residence, which can be glimpsed through the trees from around the estate. At nearby **LITTLE BADMINTON**, a fine medieval dovecote stands in the middle of a pleasant village green, alongside the church of St Michael. During the 1960s, it was fitted out with a plastic tower for the filming of *Sky West and Crooked*, directed by John Mills and starring his daughter, Hayley.

The medieval dovecote at Little Badminton

Quiet Cotswold byways

EASTON GREY

A picturesque village of Cotswold-style cottages, farms and barns, all grouped together on the riverbank above the Avon. The river is wide enough to be spanned by a handsome five-arched bridge, which adds further to the beauty of the scene. Above the village stands Easton Grey House and the village church, surrounded by fine wooded parkland that makes this an almost perfect Cotswold cameo.

RIVER AVON

The River Avon is crossed at Easton Grey, whilst a diminutive tributary stream is passed near journey's end between Alderton and Great Badminton. Some 75 miles in length, the Avon flows from a number of possible sources here in the Southwolds, down through Bath and Bristol to join the Bristol Channel at Avonmouth. One of these possible sources is Joyce's Pool, passed along the way on the fringes of Didmarton. 'Avon' is in fact a common English river name, with the Bristol, Warwickshire and Hampshire versions alone being waters of national repute. The name itself is not that original, the Celtic word *'afon'* simply meaning 'water'.

8

Marshfield, Nettleton and Castle Combe

18 miles

The Cotswold landscape is broadly divided into the wide open spaces of the upland plateau, and the shady secluded valleys that are home to sparkling rivers and picture postcard villages. This route combines the best of both worlds. Much of the ride is spent exploring the gently undulating plateau north of Bath, whilst towards journey's end, the circuit plunges downhill into the By Brook valley and Castle Combe.

Although largely an excursion through open countryside – where the open aspect will mean hard going on windy days – there are a number of attractive stone villages along the way. In addition to Castle Combe, there is the large hilltop settlement of Marshfield, the scattered village of Nettleton and the intriguingly named 'the Gibb', which was indeed the site of public executions in centuries past! The yew tree opposite the Salutation pub in this diminutive hamlet replaced the original tree that was used as the gibbet or gallows.

Map: OS Landrangers 172 Bristol and Bath and 173 Swindon and Devizes (GR 787738).

Starting point: Follow the A420 Bristol to Chippenham road as far as Marshfield. At the eastern end of Marshfield, turn off the main road along the turning that leads into the village centre. Almost immediately, turn left into a lay-by alongside the A420.

Refreshments: Along the way, there are pubs at both the Gibb and Castle Combe, whilst at journey's end in Marshfield your choice of refreshment facilities includes the Crown Inn and the Lord Nelson. If your tastes are more down-to-earth, there is usually a mobile refreshment van in the lay-by where the route starts/finishes, that sells the usual range of burgers, rolls, coffee and such like.

The route: There are one or two hills along the way, particularly in and around Castle Combe. Beyond West Littleton, the route has to cross the very busy A46 twice. This major trunk road leads to the M4 motorway, and you will have to wait patiently for gaps in the traffic. The main road can be avoided by following a rough track that runs to the east of the A46, although this is not the easiest of routes to cycle along!

---

1. From the lay-by, follow the road into the village centre at Marshfield and cycle the whole length of the High Street. At the western end of the High Street, just before a former toll-house, **turn R** at a minor crossroads – the left

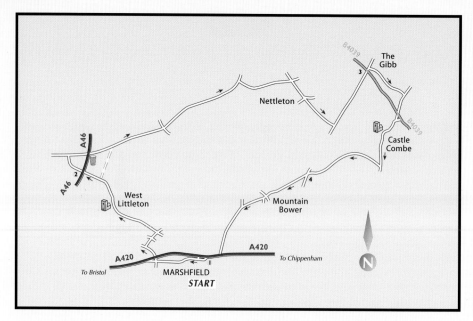

turn is called Green Lane.

Cycle up to the A420, and follow the unclassified lane opposite. In just under ½ mile, at a junction, **turn R** to pass in front of a collection of cottages that house the Marshfield Bakery. In ¼ mile, keep ahead at a crossroads following the lane signposted to West Littleton.

In 200 yards, at the next crossroads, **turn L** to continue following the lane signposted to West Littleton. This lane drops downhill before climbing up into the village. Continue along the lane beyond the village for ¾ mile to the busy A46.

2. Cross the A46 and follow the lane opposite for ½ mile to a junction, before **turning R** to return to the A46. Follow the lane opposite, alongside the Crown Inn, signposted to Burton, Nettleton and West Kington.

In 1½ miles, at a crossroads, continue ahead for 1¾ miles along the lane signposted to Burton and Nettleton, before **turning R** along a side turning signposted to Nettleton and West Kington. In 1 mile, at a staggered crossroads – the left-turn is Edgecorner Lane – **turn R** and follow a lane into Nettleton.

At the junction immediately past the post office, keep ahead on the main through road signposted to North Wraxall. In ¾ mile, at a junction, **turn L** along the lane signposted to the Gibb and Grittleton, following what is the course of the Foss Way. Follow this lane for 1¼ miles up to the B4039 and the Salutation Inn at the Gibb.

3. Follow the lane opposite signposted to Grittleton. Immediately past the Salutation Inn, **turn R** into Summer Lane. In ¾ mile, at the next junction, **turn R** to return to the B4039. **Turn L and, almost immediately, R** along the road to Castle Combe and the Visitors

Castle Combe

Car Park. In 150 yards, at the next junction, **turn R** and head downhill into Castle Combe.

Cycle through the village, across the By Brook and on uphill for ½ mile to the next junction. **Turn R** – signposted to North Wraxall – and follow this lane for 1½ miles to a crossroads.

4. Follow the lane opposite signposted to West Kington and Mountain Bower. Keep on this lane for ¾ mile to a crossroads on the far side of the hamlet of Mountain Bower. Go straight across, signposted to Marshfield. In ½ mile, at a junction, **turn L** and follow a lane for 1 mile to reach the A420. **Turn R** and, in 200 yards, a **L turn** brings you back to the lay-by where the route started.

MARSHFIELD

Do not be put off by the name. The village is located high on the Cotswold plateau, and in no way resembles a damp, low-lying, wetland environment. The name actually comes from the Old English word '*mearc*' which translated to 'boundary'. Marshfield originally lay on the main London to Bristol coach route, and it was only the arrival of the M4 motorway that led to the disappearance of heavy traffic from its attractive High Street. Flanked by 17th and 18th-century cottages, the main street through the village runs from a tollhouse and 17th-century almshouses at its western end to the triangular 'Market' at its eastern end. The Market is overlooked by Marshfield's large Perpendicular church, which dates from the 15th century and is best known

The open road near Marshfield

for its fine Jacobean pulpit. Boxing Day morning is the time to visit Marshfield, when the locals dress up in strips of paper to perform a 'Mummers' Play'. This has pagan origins, and is said to commemorate the death of winter and the rebirth of a new season.

THE BY BROOK

Castle Combe is described in route number 9. The village itself lies on the By Brook, a picturesque tributary of the Bristol Avon which it joins at Bathford on the eastern fringes of Bath. This delightful Cotswold river flows through a narrow, flat-bottomed valley, surrounded on all sides by thick deciduous woodland. This superb natural environment is home to a rich variety of wildlife and flora. Pause on the roadside by the river at the southern end of Castle Combe, and you will no doubt be able to spot the large numbers of trout that glide gently along the river bed. The By Brook valley, however, is perhaps best known for the rich variety of wildfowl that makes its home along the riverbank. The species found hereabouts include kingfishers and dippers, buzzards and woodpeckers, as well as moorhen, coot, swan and heron.

Castle Combe and Foxley

19 miles

This route through the North Wiltshire countryside takes you in and out of villages that were once the economic backbone of rural life. Now few people here make a living from the surrounding land, with the majority of residents either being retired folk or commuters to nearby towns and cities such as Bristol or Swindon. The attractions of the area are obvious, this being the Cotswold fringe with fine cottages and houses fashioned out of the golden local stone. Along the way lie a number of handsome churches, a restored Victorian school, a selection of welcoming hostelries, but above all a quite superb slice of undulating Wiltshire countryside. It is altogether perfect cycling country, with little traffic, gentle gradients and a relaxed and peaceful atmosphere.

Map: OS Landranger 173 Swindon and Devizes (GR 845778).

Starting point: The signposted public car park in Upper Castle Combe alongside the B4039 Acton Turville to Chippenham road.

Refreshments: The Vine Tree at Norton is an ideal refreshment stop. This regular entry in the *Good Pub Guide* lies well over halfway around the route, and has an excellent reputation for both its food and real ales. Hot cyclists in need of rest and refreshment will find the picnic tables in the garden an ideal place to rest awhile.

The route: This ride is gentle throughout, and any hills are either short or capable of being cycled up with little effort. Other than ¼ mile of the B4039 in Upper Castle Combe, the route is entirely on quiet unclassified lanes.

1. Leave the car park, **turn L** up to the B4039, **turn L and in 50 yards R** along the lane signposted to Grittleton. In 600 yards, at a minor crossroads, **turn L** along Summer Lane.

Follow this lane for 1 mile to a junction in the Gibb, then **turn R** to pass under the M4 motorway. In ¼ mile, by an isolated cottage, **turn L** along the Littleton Drew road.

Follow this lane for ½ mile to a junction on the southern edge of Littleton Drew. **Turn R**, pass through the village and, in ½ mile, **turn R** along the Alderton road. Follow this byway for 1¾ miles to a crossroads on the edge of Alderton.

2. Head directly across at this crossroads and cycle through Alderton, keeping on the road as it bears right past the church up to a junction. **Turn L** and,

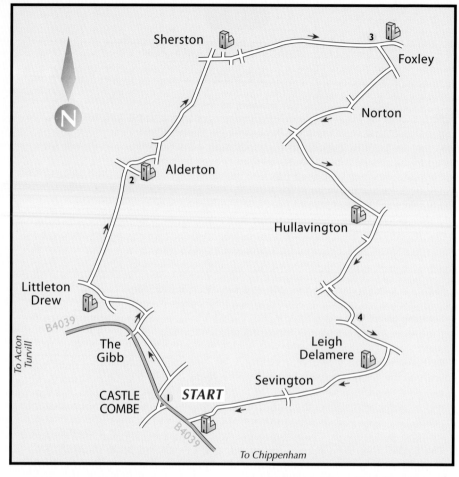

in 600 yards at the next junction, **turn R** along the road signposted to Sherston and Malmesbury.

In 1½ miles, at a crossroads just before Sherston, **turn R** along the lane signposted to Foxley and Malmesbury. In ¼ mile, **turn R** at a T-junction. In just 200 yards, **fork L** at a junction off of the main road onto a lane signposted to Foxley and Malmesbury. Follow the lane ahead for 2¼ miles into Foxley, keeping ahead at two crossroads along the way.

3. Enter Foxley and, by the green, **turn R** along the road to Norton and Hullavington. Follow this lane for 1 mile into Norton, passing the Vine Tree and a ford to reach a T-junction. **Turn R**, signposted to Sherston.

In 1 mile, where the road bears sharply right towards Sherston, keep ahead along a side lane to Farleaze. In just 75 yards, **turn L** and follow an unsigned lane for 2 miles to reach the main street in Hullavington and the Queen's Head Inn. **Turn R** and cycle through the village.

Near journey's end

In 1 mile, take the **second of two consecutive L turns** signposted to Kington St Michael and Stanton. Follow this lane for 600 yards around to a T-junction, ignoring a left turn to Hullavington along the way.

4. Turn L – signposted to Kington St Michael and Chippenham – and in ½ mile **turn R** along the road to Leigh Delamere and Sevington.

Follow this lane for 2 miles, passing through both Leigh Delamere and Sevington, to reach a crossroads. Head straight across and follow the lane opposite for 1 mile to reach the B4039 in Upper Castle Combe.

Turn R and, in ¼ mile, **turn L** along the road signposted to the car park.

CASTLE COMBE

Although the circuit bypasses the centre of Castle Combe, it is worth making a detour at journey's end to visit the village that has been used as an image on any number of greetings cards, chocolate box lids, jigsaw puzzles and biscuit tins. You will certainly experience a sense of *déjà vu* even if you have never visited the village before! The Cotswold-style cottages that sweep down from the market cross to the delightful stone bridge across the By Brook attract visitors from all over the world. Voted the 'prettiest village in England' as far back as 1962, film buffs might just recognise Castle Combe as being the setting for the 1967 version of *Dr Dolittle*.

FOXLEY AND NORTON

Although diminutive in both size and appearance, these neighbouring villages contain much of interest for the visitor. Foxley is centred upon a triangular common, overlooked by an attractive church of unknown dedication. At the eastern end of the village – just off the route – lies a tiny chapel in the heart of Courage Farm. The annual Rogationtide service held here sees most of the congregation worshipping in the farmyard, quite simply due to the lack of accommodation in the church itself! Norton consists of little more than two dozen households grouped around a ford and a lane leading to the village church. There is an exquisite manor house, dating from 1623, as well as the Vine Tree Inn. The manor has a symmetrical front with classical-styled porch, set behind an archway and pollarded lime trees.

SEVINGTON

At the western end of Sevington lies the old village school and adjoining teacher's cottage. Dating from 1849 – and closed as far back as 1913 – the school has now been restored and is used as an educational resource for local school children. Victorian desks, books, uniforms and other memorabilia are all on display, as well as a photograph of the last three boys to be educated at the school. Although not generally open to the public, Sevington School presents a handsome exterior to the passing visitor. (Telephone 01249 783070 for further information on the school.)

Norton Manor

10
Through the Vale of Pewsey

18 miles

The Vale of Pewsey remains one of the great unexplored backwaters in the south of England. Bordered to the south by Salisbury Plain and to the north by the Marlborough Downs, the vale is a rich agricultural landscape characterised by arable farming. The downs, almost whaleback in character, provide a unique backdrop throughout this circuit, with Tan Hill and Milk Hill almost reaching the 1,000 foot contour mark. It comes as no surprise to find that the tag 'Area of Outstanding Natural Beauty' has been attached to this quiet corner of Wiltshire.

This route through the Vale of Pewsey includes a number of attractive villages, where brick and thatch predominate as building materials. Each village has a tale to tell, none more so than Woodborough. Nearby Swanborough Tump was the site of a Saxon hundred court where Ethelred and Alfred the Great held a state council. It has even been suggested that Alfred made his will at the spot now marked by a commemorative plaque. In more recent times, the Kennet & Avon Canal was carved through the vale, adding yet another element of historical interest to this cycle tour through one of the most beautiful locations in Wiltshire.

Map: OS Landranger 173 Swindon and Devizes (GR 038632).

Starting point: The Bridge Inn at Horton. From the A361, on the eastern outskirts of Devizes, at a roundabout alongside a garage, turn off the main road into Horton Road. The Bridge Inn lies 1 mile along this road on the right. There is a small unmetalled lay-by opposite the pub. If this is full, turn right immediately past the Bridge Inn, and park in another unmetalled parking area 100 yards down this lane alongside the K&A Canal.

Refreshments: Along the way, there are plenty of opportunities for refreshment, with pubs at Horton, Wilcot, Woodborough and Coate. My own favourite is the Swan at Wilcot, a very pretty, old and steeply thatched hostelry. The Seven Stars at Woodborough receives an excellent review in the *Good Pub Guide*, where it is described as 'Anglo-French and thoroughly fantastic'.

The route: This route follows unclassified roads and lanes through the Vale of Pewsey, where the traffic flows are relatively light. The road from Horton through to Wilcot can be occasionally busy, being the 'main' road through the Vale of Pewsey from Devizes to Pewsey itself. As an alternative, it is possible to follow the towpath of the K&A Canal. The only problem with this route is that the surface is unmetalled, and can be waterlogged and boggy during the winter months. In the summer, it is idyllic cycling . . . if a little bumpy! The going is pretty flat throughout, although there is one steep hill as the route climbs out of Alton Barnes, and another short climb northwards out of Etchilhampton.

1. Follow the road eastwards from the Bridge Inn through the Vale of Pewsey for 4 miles, passing through Horton and Allington along the way.

In 4 miles, at a T-junction in Alton Barnes, **turn L** along the road signposted to Pewsey and Marlborough. Almost immediately, take the **R turn** signposted to Wilcot and Pewsey. Follow this road over the northern fringes of Woodborough Hill and on for another 2 miles down into Wilcot.

Cross the Kennet & Avon Canal and continue to the crossroads by the Golden Swan Inn.

(NB. An alternative is to join the K&A Canal opposite the Bridge Inn and to cycle along the towpath to Wilcot – but only in dry weather when the path is firm.)

2. Keep straight ahead, signposted to Manningford, passing the Golden Swan on the right. In 300 yards, at a junction, **keep R** along the Manningford road.

In ½ mile, at a crossroads, **turn R** along the lane signposted to Woodborough and Bottlesford. Follow the 'main' road for 2½ miles to a crossroads in the village of Woodborough, ignoring two left turns along the way. For reference, the road opposite at this crossroads is Smithy Lane – signposted to the Social Club.

Turn L, signposted to Hilcott and Upavon. Follow this road south for 600 yards, crossing a railway line, to the next junction. **Turn R** along the road signposted to Beechingstoke and Marden.

3. Follow this road for 1¼ miles into Beechingstoke, before continuing out of the village on the same road, now signposted to Patney and Devizes.

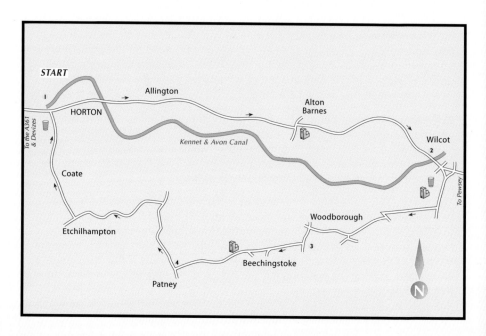

Pleasure craft on the Kennet & Avon Canal

Continue for ¾ mile to the next junction, and keep directly ahead on the road signposted to All Cannings, ignoring the left-turn to Patney.

In ¼ mile, at a T-junction, **turn R** along the road signposted to All Cannings.

4. Follow the road over the railway, before continuing for 1½ miles to the next junction. **Turn L** – signposted to Etchilhampton and Devizes – and follow this road for 1¾ miles through to the edge of Etchilhampton and a right turn to Coate.

Turn R at this point, cross the fringes of Etchilhampton Hill and drop downhill into Coate. Continue through Coate and neighbouring Little Horton before continuing for ¾ mile to a road

junction alongside the Bridge Inn.

● ●

THE KENNET & AVON CANAL

Between Devizes, Pewsey and Wootton Rivers, the canal passes through what is known as the 'Long Pound'. Without a single lock in 15 miles of waterway, this must have come as welcome relief to the bargees who had recently negotiated no fewer than 29 sets of locks on the western approaches to Devizes. Cyclists following the towpath will soon notice how the canal winds its way around such isolated hillocks as the Knoll, Woodborough Hill and Picked Hill, prominent landmarks in the Vale of Pewsey. The most noticeable features on this stretch of the canal are Ladies Bridge, with its ornate facades, and Wilcot Water, more an ornamental lake than navigable

51

waterway. Lady Wroughton of Wilcot Manor would only allow the canal to pass through her estate if it pleased her aesthetic sensibilities!

WILCOT

Wilcot is centred upon a triangular green, set about with thatched cottages of stone, brick and slate. The Kennet & Avon Canal runs to the north of the green, whilst to the south lies the 19th-century Swan Inn, as well as the original core of the village. This consists of the parish church, the manor and farm, the former vicarage and a cluster of rustic cottages. Holy Cross church, a rebuilding of 1876, stands alongside the 17th-century manor house. Those of an agile and interested disposition will be able to glimpse the manor's circular dovecote beyond the churchyard wall. Dating from 1737, this is similar to another unusual dovecote to be found at Avebury Manor.

THE ALTON BARNES WHITE HORSE

On the south-facing slopes of the Marlborough Downs to the north of this route, and standing some 650 feet above sea level, the horse is said to be visible from Old Sarum near Salisbury, 20 miles away. It was cut in 1812, at the expense of a Mr Robert Pile of Alton Barnes, who paid a journeyman painter £20 to carry out the task. John Thorpe, nicknamed Jack the Painter, was foolishly paid in advance. He promptly disappeared! He was later hanged for some unknown crime, leaving Pile with the task of finishing the horse himself. Such is the stuff of which legends are made!

Swanborough Tump

11

Through the Vale of Steeple Ashton

19 miles

Between the Wiltshire towns of Trowbridge and Devizes, a number of attractive red-brick villages lie scattered across what is known geographically as the Vale of Steeple Ashton. These include Steeple Ashton itself, as well as Keevil, Bulkington, Poulshot and Rowde. A network of generally quiet lanes connects these villages, which are all the better for being off the main tourist routes. Running parallel, the return route follows the Kennet and Avon Canal, arguably the finest artificial waterway in the south of England. Along this section of the canal there are locks aplenty, including the Caen Hill staircase of 16 consecutive locks that carry the K&A up into Devizes.

Map: OS Landranger 173 Swindon and Devizes (GR 871593).

Starting point: Hilperton church on the fringes of Trowbridge. Take the A361 east from Trowbridge, before turning off onto the B3105 into Hilperton. Turn left opposite the Lion and Fiddle public house, followed by the second turning on the left into the Knap. This leads up to the church, where there is ample roadside parking.

Refreshments: You will undoubtedly pause for refreshment at the Barge Inn at Seend, a delightful canalside watering hole. This is just 5 miles from the end of this cycle tour, and there could be few better places to enjoy refreshment than sat at one of the picnic tables alongside the K&A.

The route: Once the ever-growing eastern suburbs of Trowbridge have been left behind, this route follows flat and predominantly quiet lanes across an area known in the local guidebooks as the Vale of Steeple Ashton. The busy A361 does have to be crossed on a couple of occasions, whilst the B3101 leading into Rowde can be fairly busy at times. Beyond Rowde, the route follows the towpath of the Kennet and Avon Canal back to Whaddon, where a short stretch of country lane brings the circuit back into Hilperton. The towpath has a made-up surface that is good for cycling, but do keep an eye out for the occasional rogue piece of gravel which could puncture your tyre.

---

1. Return to the B3105, **turn R** and cycle up to the road junction by the Lion and Fiddle public house. **Turn L** and, in 100 yards, **R** into Ashton Road, a cul-de-sac. Where this cul-de-sac ends, continue ahead along a tarmac path to join a road in the new Paxcroft Mead Estate.

Continue down to a roundabout, the

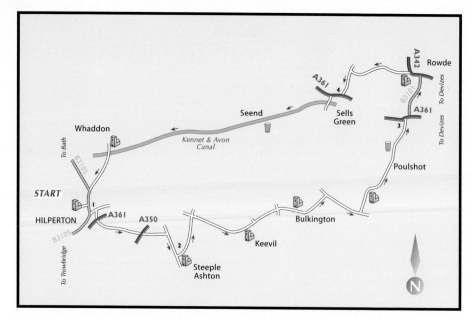

junction with the A361, and keep directly ahead along the road signposted to West Ashton and Keevil. Follow this road – Ashton Road – to its junction with the A350 and a set of traffic lights.

Follow the road opposite signposted to Steeple Ashton and Keevil Airfield. In ½ mile, at the next junction, **turn R** along the road to Steeple Ashton. Follow this road uphill for ½ mile until you come to Steeple Ashton.

2. On entering the village, take the **first L turn** signposted to Keevil and Seend, with views to the right of Salisbury Plain.

In 1 mile, at the next junction, **turn R** along the road signposted to Keevil and Bulkington. Follow this lane for 3 miles, passing through both Keevil and Bulkington, ignoring all side turns along the way.

At the junction ½ mile beyond Bulkington, **turn R** along the road signposted to Worton. In ¾ mile, **turn L** along the Poulshot road. Follow this road for 2½ miles, passing through Poulshot, before reaching the busy A361 road running from Melksham to Devizes.

3. **Turn R** and, in just 100 yards, **turn L** along the B3101 signposted to Rowde. Follow this road over the K&A Canal – the Caen Hill locks on the right – and on for 1 mile to its junction with the A342 by the Cross Keys pub in Rowde.

Turn L and, just past the George and Dragon pub, **fork L** onto a minor side road by the village shop. Follow this lane ahead – it is shortly signposted as the Common – to a junction in 1½ miles at the top end of the Common. **Turn L** along the road signposted to Seend, and continue for ¾ mile to the A361.

A delightful watering hole en route

4. Turn R – the road is signposted to Melksham – and in just 100 yards, just before the Three Magpies pub in Sells Green, **turn L** along a side lane. In 100 yards, just before a canal bridge, pass through a gate on the right to join the towpath. **Turn R**, and follow the K&A Canal towpath in a westerly direction for 5 miles to bridge number 163 near Whaddon.

Just before this bridge, **bear R** up to Whaddon Lane. **Turn L**, and follow this lane for 1 mile to the B3105 in Hilperton. **Turn L** and, in just 150 yards, **turn R** back into the Knap.

● ● ● ● ● ● ● ● ● ● ● ● ● ● ● ● ● ● ● ●

THE KENNET AND AVON CANAL
On the western edge of Devizes, the route crosses the Kennet and Avon Canal

at the foot of the Caen Hill staircase of 16 consecutive locks. Alongside each lock is a water-storage side-pond, which attracts a wide range of wildfowl. The perfect symmetry of this wonder of the waterways system led to L.T.C. Rolt describing Caen Hills as 'the most spectacular lock flight in England'.

Along the 5-mile stretch of towpath followed on this route, there are also smaller flights of locks at both Semington and Seend. Semington is also the location of a diminutive aqueduct that carries the K&A across Semington Brook, as well as the long defunct junction of the K&A with the Wiltshire and Berkshire Canal. The W&B headed north from this junction to join the River Thames at Abingdon.

55

A quiet stretch of the Kennet & Avon Canal

KEEVIL

Keevil is a picturesque village full of quite charming brick and timber-framed properties. The 15th-century battlemented church possesses a fine nave roof with painted timbers, whilst the churchyard is full of magnificent carved tombstones. The local manor dates from the late 16th century, and is located in the parkland near to the church. In centuries past, Anne Beach, daughter of the Lord of the Manor, fell in love with a William Winahouse, the local curate. Her father, disapproving of the relationship, locked her in a room over the porch of the manor for over two years. She was eventually given the choice of leaving her lover or losing her inheritance. She chose to marry, but died within three months.

POULSHOT

East of Keevil is the long straggling village of Poulshot, whose public house – the Raven – lies a mile to the north of the local church. The delightful village green is home to the local cricket club, and is really the most perfect spot to watch England's traditional summer game. What could be more idyllic than a game of cricket played out against a backdrop of brick cottages, lines of trees and the distant skyline of Salisbury Plain?

12

Holt, Lacock and Broughton Gifford

20 miles

Imagine a route that contained no fewer than three National Trust properties – it must be something special! This circuit around West Wiltshire offers just that. At Holt, there is the Courts Garden; at Lacock, the abbey founded back in the 12th century; at Great Chalfield, a fine 15th-century manor.

The natural landscape is pleasant, with the occasional gradient bringing its reward in the form of far-ranging views across the Wiltshire countryside. This is particularly the case during the early stages of the ride, as the route climbs gently from Holt to Atworth and on towards Neston. Beyond, the circuit descends almost imperceptibly into the Avon Vale, with the River Avon itself being crossed at picturesque bridges in Reybridge and Lacock. Lacock will surely be an irresistible resting place along the way, even if the abbey does not feature on your agenda. The brick and timber properties that line the village streets are an absolute delight.

Map: OS Landranger 173 Swindon and Devizes (GR 862618).

Starting point: The car park in Holt. Holt lies 2½ miles east of Bradford-on-Avon on the B3107 road to Melksham. In the village, turn left into the Midlands by the Holt Superstore. The car park lies just a short distance along this side turning.

Refreshments: There are refreshment opportunities aplenty along the way, with Lacock offering the most appealing choice of hostelries and tearooms. Both the George and the Red Lion in Lacock earn primary entries in the *Good Pub Guide*, and come highly recommended. Towards journey's end, the Bell on the Common in Broughton Gifford is a splendid spot to rest and enjoy a drink, whilst back in Holt, both the Ham Tree and the Toll Gate offer excellent opportunities for refreshment.

The route: There are a few climbs along the way, but none with any significant gradients. The A363 has to be crossed at Atworth, whilst the busy A350 trunk route has to be crossed on two occasions near Lacock. Do not let these negative points dissuade you, however, because most of the route lies along quiet lanes and byways with relatively light volumes of traffic . . . and for every uphill stretch there is a compensatory downhill section of roadway.

1. Return to the B3107, **turn R**, cycle through Holt to the Toll Gate Inn and **turn R** along the road signposted to Great Chalfield.

Follow this road for 1¼ miles, ignoring two right turns to Great Chalfield along the way, until you reach a right turn signposted to Atworth. **Turn R,**

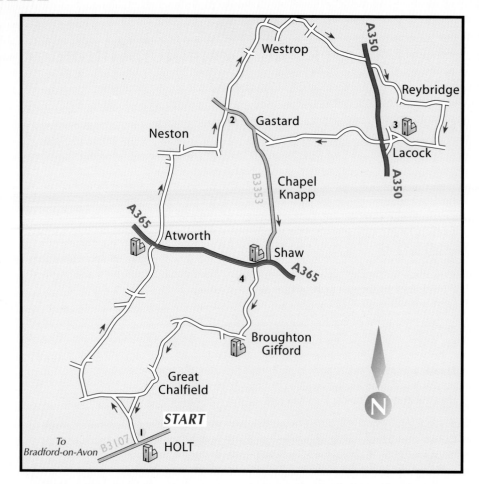

and follow this road for 1½ miles to a T-junction. **Turn R**, and follow the next section of road for ¾ mile into Atworth, where the road bears right to join the A365.

Turn L along the main road and, almost immediately, **turn R** along the road signposted to Neston. Follow this road for 1½ miles to a T-junction in front of a property, ignoring an earlier left turn called Chapel Lane.
At this junction, **turn R** along the road signposted to The Ridge and Corsham. Ignoring one early left turn, keep ahead across The Ridge and, where Green Road comes in from the right, **bear L** down Monks Lane to reach the B3353.

2. Cross the B3353, and follow Ladbrook Lane opposite signposted to Westrop and Chippenham. In 1 mile, at a crossroads, keep straight ahead and continue into the hamlet of Westrop.

In 300 yards beyond Westrop, **keep R** at an unsigned junction and follow the lane down to a T-junction in the farming hamlet of Easton.

Medieval Lacock

Turn L and, in ¼ mile, **R** at a crossroads along the road signposted to Lacock. Follow this road for 1½ miles to the A350. **Turn R** and, almost immediately, **L** along the turning signposted to Reybridge. Follow this lane for ¾ mile into Reybridge, **turn L** and cross the Avon and, in ½ mile, **turn R** at an unsigned junction. Follow this lane in a southerly direction past Bewley Court and Bewley Common to the next junction by the Bell Inn in ½ mile.

Turn R, and follow the road across the Avon and on into Lacock. On reaching the junction on the edge of the village, dismount and follow the 'No entry' road ahead the short distance into the centre of Lacock.

3. Continue to the end of the High Street, and **turn L** along the road signposted to Melksham, Devizes and Trowbridge. Continue up to a roundabout, keep ahead and almost immediately **turn R** into Folly Lane East.

Cross the A350 at the end of this cul-de-sac lane – it is reached via a short section of tarmac path – and continue along Folly Lane West signposted to Gastard.

Follow this lane for 2 miles, ignoring all side turns, to join the B3353 in Gastard by the Harp and Crown Inn. **Turn L** and follow the B3353 up to Chapel Knapp, before continuing downhill for 1½ miles to its junction with the A365 in Whitley. **Turn R** – the road is signposted to Bath.

4. In ¼ mile, take the **L turn** signposted to Norrington and Broughton Gifford. Follow this lane across Norrington Common and on to a junction in 1¼ miles. **Turn R**, and follow the road into Broughton Gifford, past the Bell and on across the Common.

A ¼ mile out of the village, **turn L** along the lane to Great Chalfield. Follow the tree-lined avenue for ¾ mile to Chalfield Manor, **bear L** in front of the manor house and continue along the lane for ½ mile to a **L turn** signposted to Holt and Trowbridge.

Turn L, passing Holt Manor, and continue to a junction by a lodge. **Turn L** down into Holt, rejoin the B3107 by the Toll Gate and **turn L** to return to the car park.

● ●

HOLT

Holt really is a village of great contrasts. Driving along the main road, passing motorists glimpse Ham Green, overlooked by a number of impressive dwellings, and the entrance to the Courts, the National Trust property where a local magistrate would have adjudicated in disputes between local weavers. Just off the main road, however, lies the Midlands, where red-brick factory buildings present a picture more akin with the Industrial Revoluton. The buildings have over the years been used for a range of purposes, including leather finishing and dyeing, and bedding

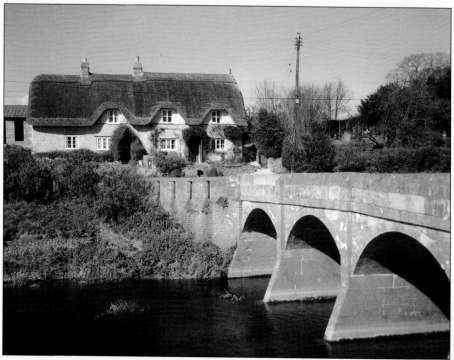

Reybridge

Chalfield Manor

manufacturing. Holt has a long industrial history. It was here in 1838 that the first Chartist meeting in Wiltshire was held, at a time of economic depression when the local clothing industry was in decline.

GREAT CHALFIELD

The village is dominated by its 15th-century manor house, now a National Trust property. Built by Thomas Trapnell in 1480, the manor sits alongside All Saints church with its delightful projecting bellcote. The grouping of fine old buildings overlooking the moat, deep in the Wiltshire countryside, is quite perfect, especially when reached by way of a tree-lined avenue that stretches for some ¾ mile. It will prove to be an absolute must for photographers . . . so remember that camera!

LACOCK

Lacock has been described as 'easily the most remarkable and the most beautiful village in Wiltshire'. Based around four streets – Church Street, West and East Streets and the High Street – the village still very much resembles a medieval town. Attractive houses cover every century from the 13th through to the 18th, with little more recent development to spoil the overall effect. Even the telephone box is an unobtrusive shade of grey. There is so much to see in Lacock – its abbey, the Fox Talbot Museum of Photography, St Cyriac's church, the tithe barn, the village cross, the packhorse bridge, and so on – that the interested visitor is advised to visit the National Trust shop in the High Street to purchase a copy of the Trust's guide to the village.

Bradford-on-Avon

16 miles

This is a magnificent ride through the heart of the Avon Valley between Bradford-on-Avon and the fringes of Bath. The outward leg of the journey takes you high above the River Avon, across the eastern hilltops of the valley. Despite the tree cover afforded by Warleigh Wood, there are occasional glimpses across the valley towards Claverton Manor, now home to the American Museum.

Having dropped down to Batheaston and Bathampton at the northern end of the valley, the ride joins the Kennet and Avon Canal whose towpath is followed back to Bradford-on-Avon. This is level cycling all the way, which presents the opportunity to cross what is undoubtedly the finest aqueduct in Southern England at Dundas, before returning to Bradford-on-Avon, one of England's finest small towns.

Map: OS Landrangers 173 Swindon and Devizes and 172 Bath and Bristol (GR 824607).

Starting point: The station car park in Bradford-on-Avon. This lies in the centre of the town, and is signposted off the A363 Bath to Trowbridge road.

Refreshments: Halfway around the route at Bathampton, the George Inn alongside the K&A Canal provides an ideal refreshment stop. Back in Bradford-on-Avon, there are any number of pubs, cafes and teashops that cater for the town's many visitors.

The route: Getting out of Bradford-on-Avon is not easy. There is a short section of busy road, followed by one very steep hill that all but the 'King of the Mountains' will choose to walk. Within ½ mile, however, these difficulties will be forgotten.

---

1. Leave the station car park and **turn L** to follow the busy A363 into the centre of Bradford-on-Avon. Once across the town bridge that crosses the River Avon, **turn L** at the mini-roundabout to continue along the A363 up out of the town centre.

In 150 yards, where the main road bears right, **turn L** into Newtown, an unclassified road signposted to Turleigh and Avoncliff. In just 75 yards, **turn R** into Conigre Hill and follow this very steep lane uphill for 200 yards to join the B3108. Cross over into Huntingdon Street, and follow this lane directly ahead for 200 yards until it joins the Ashley Road.

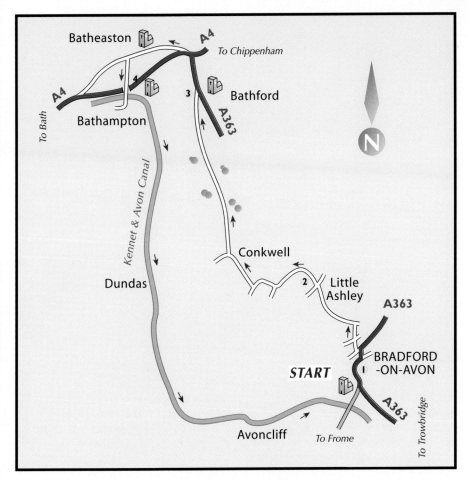

Turn **L**, and follow Ashley Road for ¾ mile to the crossroads at Little Ashley, passing the Dog and Fox pub along the way.

2. Follow the lane ahead signposted to Conkwell and Haugh for 1 mile until you reach a **R turn** signposted 'Conkwell ¾ mile'. Ignore all other side turnings along the way. Follow this lane to the right, away from Conkwell, for ½ mile to the next **R turn**, and follow this side lane to the right as it passes through Warleigh Wood.

Continue down this very steep lane until you reach the A363 on the edge of Bathford. This is **a dangerous junction**, but a mirror opposite will enable you to see traffic coming from the right.

3. **Turn L**, and follow the A363 for ½ mile to its junction with the A4, immediately past a railway overbridge. **Just before** this junction, **turn L** to follow the footway/cycleway underneath the A4 and up to the entrance to the Duck and Punt Restaurant.

Bradford Wharf

Join Batheaston High Street – the former A4 which has now been bypassed – just past the restaurant entrance, and **turn L**. Follow this road through Batheaston for ½ mile, before **turning L** along the road signposted 'Toll Bridge – Bathampton and Warminster'.

Follow this road across the toll bridge – cyclists free – and on over the A4 and the railway up to the Kennet & Avon Canal towpath alongside the primary school in Bathampton. The George Inn is conveniently located to the right.

4. Join the towpath in front of Bathampton Junior School and **turn L**, cycling away from the fringes of Bath.

In 3 miles, just before Dundas Wharf,

cross a bridge across the canal to join the towpath on the opposite bank. Cycle around the perimeter of Dundas Wharf, cross the entrance to the Somerset Coal Canal and continue following the towpath as it crosses Dundas Aqueduct.

Continue along the towpath for 2½ miles to Avoncliff Aqueduct, cross the Avon and immediately follow the lane **to the R** that passes beneath the aqueduct. Continue up to the Cross Guns Inn, **bear R** and rejoin the towpath.

Follow the towpath **to the L** for 1½ miles to the Lock Keeper Cottage and the B3109 in Bradford-on-Avon. **Turn L** and, in ¼ mile, a **L turn** returns you to the car park.

Dundas Wharf

BRADFORD-ON-AVON

Originally a 'broad ford' through the River Avon, the Saxon town of Bradford-on-Avon has been responsible for the launch of any number of postcards, television programmes, books and magazines. With its serried ranks of weavers' cottages lining the hillside above the Avon, all fashioned from the local golden limestone, the town really is a picture when illuminated by the rays of a setting sun. It is not difficult to see why the guidebooks describe the town as being a 'clone of Bath'.

The town's architecture is something special. The Saxon church, the lock up in the middle of the town bridge, the vast tithe barn, the Shambles and Dutch Barton are just some of the magnificent buildings about which many a lengthy tome has been written. Any visitors interested in discovering more about the history of this delightful small town should visit the local museum, housed above the library in the centre of Bradford-on-Avon.

THE KENNET AND AVON CANAL

When canal mania swept through Britain in the late 18th century, it did not go unnoticed even in the normally sedate West Country. In 1794, Royal Assent was given to a waterway that would link Bath with Newbury, an artificial cut which would provide a route for waterborne traffic between Bristol and London. By 1810, work on the Caen Hill Locks at Devizes had been completed, and the *Bath Herald* was able to report that 'the guns were fired on Sydney Wharf alongside the canal's headquarters' to celebrate the opening of the canal.

Between Bath and Bradford-on-Avon, the canal passes through the magnificent Avon Valley, where steeply wooded hillsides tumble down to the riverbank. This section of the canal can boast two of the finest aqueducts in Southern Britain, at Dundas and Avoncliff, both of which carry the waterway across the River Avon. Dundas is also the junction of the K&A with the Somerset Coal Canal, whose first 400 yards have been restored to provide moorings for the many pleasure craft that cruise the waterway at an unhurried four miles an hour.

14

Norton St Philip, Beckington and Mells

18 miles

The Mendip Hills east of Wells may lose much of the drama to be found further west, but this is an undulating landscape, with ups and downs aplenty, fortunately few of which are too severe or punishing. This circuit explores the fringes of East Mendip, between Norton St Philip, Beckington and Mells. There are several villages along the way, each of which has buildings of great antiquity with many a tale to tell. Above all, there is the natural landscape, open and rolling. A very traditional agricultural landscape worked by family farmers whose businesses can be traced back through many generations.

Map: OS Landrangers 172 Bristol and Bath and 183 Yeovil and Frome are both required for this circuit and ½ mile also creeps onto sheet 173 Swindon and Devizes (GR 772557).

Starting point: In Vicarage Lane, alongside the church in Norton St Philip, a turning south off the A366.

Refreshments: There are many pubs and inns along the route, with Rode, Beckington and Buckland Dinham all having welcoming hostelries. The best pubs, however, are the Talbot Inn at Mells and the George at Norton St Philip, both of which appear to have season tickets to the *Good Pub Guide*. Both these inns are historic buildings in their own right, dating back over many centuries.

The route: There are hills aplenty along the way, particularly between Lullington and Hardington. Whilst these hills will be within the abilities of fairly active cyclists, this route is best avoided by younger children. Most of the route follows quiet unclassified roads, but there is the occasional busy stretch of highway to be negotiated. The unclassified road running between Great Elm and Mells can be surprisingly busy during the working week, with vehicles moving to and from the local quarries.

1. Cycle back down Vicarage Lane, **turn R** and follow the A366 up to its junction with the B3110 by the George Inn. **Turn R**, and follow the B3110 through Norton St Philip for 400 yards before **turning L** into Tellisford Lane.

Follow this lane for ¾ mile to the A36.

Cross WITH EXTREME CARE and continue along Tellisford Lane for ¾ mile to a minor crossroads on the edge of Tellisford.

Turn R, and follow the lane to Rode, reaching a junction on the edge of the village by the Mill Inn in ¾ mile. **Turn**

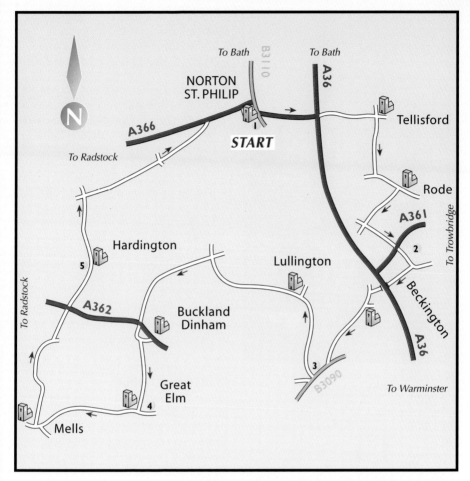

L, and cycle up Rode Hill for 300 yards before **turning R** at a minor crossroads into Rode's High Street.

Cycle through Rode and, at a crossroads some 600 yards beyond the village, **turn L** along the lane signposted to Rudge. Follow this lane for ½ mile to the A361.

2. Cross the A361 WITH CARE and continue along the lane opposite signposted to Rudge. In ½ mile, at a junction, **turn R** towards Beckington.

Follow this lane down to the junction with the Bath Road in the centre of Beckington, **turn L** and at the roundabout by the Woolpack, keep ahead along the Frome Road for 1¼ miles until you reach the B3090. **Turn R** and, in 200 yards, take the **first R** signposted to Lullington.

3. Follow this lane for 2½ miles, passing through Lullington along the way whilst avoiding all side turns.

At 1¼ miles beyond Lullington, at a

67

Mells Manor seen from the churchyard

Follow this lane as it climbs up out of Mells to join the A362 in 2 miles, ignoring the right turn to Buckland Dinham at the top of Conduit Hill.

Turn R along the A362 and, in just 100 yards, **turn L** along the lane signposted to Hardington. Follow this road – Pillar Lane – for 1 mile down to the farms that make up the diminutive hamlet of Hardington.

5. Continue along the lane up out of Hardington to reach a crossroads in 1¼ miles. **Turn R** – to Norton St Philip and Laverton – and follow the lane for 1½ miles to the next crossroads. Keep ahead – signposted Norton St Philip – for ½ mile to reach the A366.

Turn R, and head downhill for ½ mile into Norton St Philip. The **first R turn** in the village is Vicarage Lane.

● ●

NORTON ST PHILIP

Norton St Philip stands on the side of a steep hill, with its tall Perpendicular church in a hollow below the village. Norton's prosperity was founded upon the West of England cloth trade, with the village once being the home of an annual cloth fair that attracted merchants from far and wide. The attractive streets in the village are lined with handsome grey stone houses, with the inevitable focus being on the George Inn, reputedly the oldest licensed house in England. S.P.B. Mais commented, 'Its long, steep, stone roof, half-timberings, projecting windows and beams, outside stone staircase, handsome stone arch and medieval gallery in the yard, from which plays were watched, combine to make this one of the most memorable of English inns.' For once, the plethora of adjectives fail to exaggerate!

crossroads, **turn L** and follow a lane called Cock Road for 1½ miles to the A362 in Buckland Dinham by the Bell Inn.

Cross the main road and follow the road opposite – Sandcross Lane – which soon drops steeply out of the village. In ¼ mile, just before some farm buildings, **turn R** along the lane signposted to Great Elm and Mells. Follow this lane for 1 mile up to a junction in Great Elm.

4. **Turn R**, and follow the road for 1¼ miles through Great Elm and down into Mells. At the first junction in Mells, **turn R** and, almost immediately, **R again** into the lane that runs alongside the village shop.

LULLINGTON

Lullington is quite literally the gateway to the nearby Orchardleigh House, a once proud mansion set in acres of parkland which has now fallen prey to the golf course developers. In the centre of the village stands a neat green, overlooked by attractive estate-workers' cottages, the former school and All Saints church. The north doorway of the church receives praise from all of the guidebook writers as a superb example of Norman symbolism. Amongst its embellishments are a number of animals, some grotesque heads and a figure of Christ.

MELLS

Mells was originally just one small part of the far-flung empire of Glastonbury Abbey. New Street, with its medieval terraces

leading to St Andrew's church, is an arm of what was intended to be a cruciform street layout. Designed by Abbot Selwood in 1470, it has been likened to a village counterpart of Vicar's Close in Wells. At the Dissolution, the estate passed into the hands of the Horner family. Local tradition maintains that the Manor of Mells is none other than 'the plum' in the 'Little Jack Horner' nursery rhyme. The tale holds that Jack Horner was steward to Abbot Richard Whiting at the time of the Dissolution. Jack was dispatched to London with the deeds to a number of manors that were part of the rich demesne of the Abbey, all in an attempt to placate Henry VIII. Jack Horner held back one of the deeds for himself, which turned out to be none other than Mells Manor – 'he put in his thumb and pulled out a plum!'

Norton St Philip

15

Twerton, Compton Dando and Stanton Prior

14 miles

This is a route of great contrasts, as it moves from urban Bath to suburban Saltford before heading south to explore the rolling countryside of North Somerset. The first few miles follow the Bristol and Bath Railway Path, constructed on the trackbed of the former Midland Railway between these two cities. This is the heart of the Avon Valley, a river whose waters are crossed several times along the way. Then soon it is rural Somerset all the way, with villages and hamlets scattered amongst the rolling hills and sheltered valleys of this delightful landscape. Even the place names – Compton Dando and Chewton Keynsham, Burnett and Stanton Prior – have a decidedly rural sound to them! There are ups and downs along the way – steep ups and downs – which means that this is not a ride for the faint hearted. The rewards, however, in terms of far-ranging views and vistas, are worth every bead of perspiration.

Map: OS Landranger 172 Bristol and Bath (GR 725647).

Starting point: Park in Twerton's High Street – or one of the adjoining side roads – in the vicinity of Bath City's football ground. Twerton lies on the western fringes of Bath, just off the A36 Lower Bristol Road.

Refreshments: There are a number of pubs and inns along the way, with the Wheatsheaf Inn between Burnett and Stanton Prior being a convenient resting-place, well over halfway around the route.

The route: This is one of the more strenuous routes in the book, with a steep climb into Burnett and also out of Stanton Prior. Both climbs will inevitably be beyond the capabilities of all but the fittest of cyclists, so be prepared to push your cycle up these hills! There is a well-deserved reward at journey's end, however, with a lengthy descent from the hilltops above Stanton Prior back down into Twerton. A number of busy roads have to be crossed although the greater part of the route does follow quiet country lanes or suburban roads, with the added bonus of a 3-mile stretch of the car-free Bristol and Bath Railway Path.

1. Cycle along Twerton's High Street in the direction of Bath's city centre and, immediately before the newsagent's on the left and almost opposite the Old Crown pub, take a **L turn** down Mill Lane.

Pass under a railway bridge to reach the

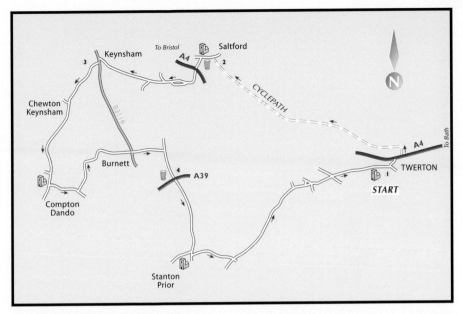

A4. **Turn R** and, in 200 yards, **turn L** by the Golden Fleece pub along the path signposted to 'Bristol and Bath Railway Path'.

Cross the footbridge over the River Avon and follow the tarmac path by the river downstream (i.e. to the left) for 600 yards until, just past the Dolphin Inn, Brassmill Lane is joined. Follow this road for 600 yards to the start of the Bristol and Bath Railway Path. Follow this for 3 miles until you come to the third bridge that crosses the River Avon.

2. Cross the river, and follow the sloping path **on the R** at the far side of the bridge down to a lane. **Turn L** under the railway bridge, and cycle up past the Bird in Hand pub in Saltford. Continue along the High Street for ¼ mile before **turning L** opposite Brunel's Tunnel House Hotel into Beach Road.

Cycle up to the A4, and cross over into

Manor Road. Follow Manor Road for ½ mile, bearing right along the way, until you reach the entrance to the Manor Lawns estate. At this point, **fork L** off the estate road onto a quiet side lane. Follow this lane for ¼ mile until it rejoins the estate road, before keeping ahead for 100 yards.

Where the main road bears right, keep ahead – actually a **L turn** off the main road – along Manor Road. In ¼ mile, having passed Keynsham Manor and Manor Farm, **turn R** at a T-junction and follow a lane for ¾ mile through to the B3116 in Keynsham.

3. Turn L and, in 150 yards, **turn R** along the lane by a telephone box signposted to Chewton and Compton Dando. Drop downhill to Chewton, cross the River Chew and continue along the road through Chewton Keynsham and on into Compton Dando, ignoring all side turns along the way.

One of the fine views from the Railway Path

In Compton Dando, **turn L** just before the Compton Inn along Bathford Hill, signposted to Marksbury, Bath and Stanton Prior. Continue on uphill for ½ mile to a junction, and **turn L** onto a minor side lane. Follow this lane for 1 mile through to the B3116 in Burnett, climbing one very steep hill just before reaching the village.

Cross the B3116 and follow the lane opposite – Middle Piece Lane – for ½ mile to a T-junction. **Turn R**, and head downhill for ½ mile to the Wheatsheaf Inn and the A39.

4. Cross the main road, and follow the lane opposite towards Stanton Prior. Climb the eastern flanks of Stantonbury Hill and drop downhill towards the village. On entering

Stanton Prior, **turn L** immediately past Poplar Farm along the lane signposted to Wilmington.

Follow this lane for ¾ mile to a crossroads high on the hilltop at the end of a steep climb. **Turn L** – signposted to Newton St Loe. Follow the hilltop road down to Pennyquick Road which is reached in 2 miles, ignoring left turns along the way and keeping ahead at one minor crossroads. **Turn R** and, in 100 yards, **turn L** into Newton Road. This turning is signposted to Twerton, the centre of which is reached in ½ mile.

● ● ● ● ● ● ● ● ● ● ● ● ● ● ● ● ● ● ●

THE BRISTOL AND BATH RAILWAY PATH

The path was constructed on the

trackbed of the former Midland Railway running between Bristol Temple Meads and Bath Green Park. Closed to passenger traffic during the Beeching era, the railway finally closed to freight traffic in 1976. For three years, the trackbed lay dormant before being converted into the Railway Path between 1979 and 1986. With its 3-metre wide tarmac surface and a level gradient, the Path makes for perfect cycling through the Avon Valley between Bath and Bristol.

COMPTON DANDO

On the River Chew between Chew Magna and Keynsham, the village enjoys a fine setting amongst the rolling hills of North Somerset, although whether cyclists fully appreciate these hills is another matter! There are a few houses, an inn and the village church, but little more. It is worth making a detour to explore St Mary's church, however, and not just to appreciate the Perpendicular tower. Inside the church, part of a Roman altar lies inserted into the foot of the north-east buttress of the chancel. The stone, believed to have been found during excavations at the Roman Baths in Bath, is carved with the figures of Roman gods.

STANTON PRIOR

Stanton Prior was part of the estates of the Priory at Bath until the Dissolution, the arms of Bath Abbey still remaining on a boss in the local church. This is one village that really does deserve to be described as idyllic, with its stone-built cottages and farmhouses surrounded by precious little modern development. Overshadowing Stanton Prior is Stantonbury Hill, site of an Iron Age fort whose remains are skirted by the Wansdyke, a frontier of bank and ditch that dates back to the 5th century when the Britons were rallying against the invading Saxons.

Heytesbury, Grovely Wood and the Wylye Valley

25 miles

The River Wylye is one of those clear chalk streams so beloved of the fly fisherman. In its clear waters, sheltering behind stones and roots, lie the somewhat solitary and sedentary trout. The Wylye has its source just above Kington Deverill, from where it flows in a north-easterly direction to Warminster before heading south-east towards its confluence with the River Nadder at Wilton. Chalk downland rises above the Wylye Valley, providing a fine backdrop to this delightful corner of Wiltshire.

This route follows the Wylye Valley from Heytesbury through Wylye as far south as Great Wishford. The villages in the valley are an absolute delight, with brick, timber and thatch cottages sitting alongside historic churches and traditional inns. By way of contrast, the circuit climbs the downs to the east of the Wylye Valley to explore the ancient glades and tracks of Grovely Wood.

Map: OS Landranger 184 Salisbury and the Plain (GR 925426).

Starting point: The main street in Heytesbury, alongside the Red Lion and the church. Follow the A36 to the roundabout at the southern end of the Warminster bypass where this trunk route is joined by the B3414. A minor road leading off the roundabout is signposted to Heytesbury.

Refreshments: There is no shortage of pubs in the Wylye Valley, with five of the villages along the way boasting fine inns with a good reputation for the quality of their food and beers. The Angel at Heytesbury receives a 'main' entry in the *Good Pub Guide*, whilst the Dove at Corton, the Carriers at Stockton and the Bell at Wylye all receive secondary entries. My own favourite – the Royal Oak at Great Wishford – doesn't even rate a mention!

The route: There is one long steep ascent from the valley bottom at Wylye up to Grovely Wood, but this is matched by a long descent from this hilltop woodland into Great Wishford. The track through Grovely Wood, incidentally, although metalled is rough and pot-holed in places.

---

1. Follow the side turning by the church in Heytesbury signposted to Tytherington. In 600 yards, take a **L** turn – no signpost – and, in another ¼ mile, at a fork by a farm, **bear R** before following a lane for 1 mile up to a crossroads.

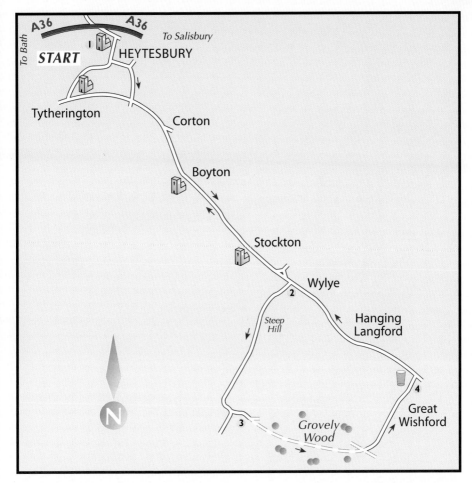

Turn L, following the unclassified road through the Wylye Valley, ignoring all side turns along the way. In 6 miles, having passed under the A303, this road reaches the village of Wylye.

2. As you enter Wylye, **bear R** into the delightfully named Teapot Street – signposted to Hanging Langford and Dinton. In 150 yards, at a junction by the United Reformed church, continue straight ahead along Fore Street. In 100 yards, **turn R** into Dinton Road, signposted to Dinton.

Follow this lane steeply out of Wylye to reach a mobile phone mast on the hilltop in 1½ miles. Continue past this tower towards some woodland. Shortly, the road bears sharply left and then sharply right. On the right-hand bend, **keep directly ahead** following a rough lane into the woodland itself.

3. Follow this track for 600 yards to a barn. Keep to the right of this barn to reach a gate and a Forestry Commission *Grovely Wood* sign.

The church of St James, Tytherington

Follow the somewhat rough road through the woodland for 2½ miles to reach a wooden barrier. Beyond this barrier – with a farm in the trees on the right – continue along a metalled lane for ¼ mile to a crossroads by a small triangular green.

Follow the lane ahead – there is an early unmetalled section – for 1¾ miles as it drops downhill to Great Wishford and the Royal Oak pub.

4. Turn L immediately past the Royal Oak, and follow the road through the Wylye Valley for 4½ miles to Wylye. Keep **to the L** of the United Reformed church in Fore Street and continue along the lane back to Corton and on to the junction passed early on in the ride, where a right turn would lead

back to Heytesbury. Ignore this turning, and keep on the lane ahead for ½ mile through to Tytherington.

Turn R at the junction by Church Farm and St James church – signposted to Heytesbury – and follow the lane for 1 mile back to Heytesbury church.

● ●

HEYTESBURY

Heytesbury was a noted cloth-making centre back in the 18th century, with two fairs being held in the main street each year. To this day, Heytesbury exudes the appearance of a small town, with its pair of hostelries and rows of attractive cottages, its almshouses and prominent church, and a main street which broadens to form what are known as 'places'. St Peter and St Paul's church is a

Grovely Wood

splendid place, cruciform in layout and with an impressive central tower. The chantry chapel was built and endowed by the Hungerford family, who also founded the local almshouses, officially known as the 'Hospital of St John in Heytesbury'. After fighting at Agincourt in 1415, Walter Hungerford, in 1419, became Steward of the Household of Henry V, and he became Treasurer of England in 1428.

WYLYE
Wylye has been described as 'a mixture of the picturesque, the ordinary and the indifferent'. The picturesque part is undoubtedly the attractive area around the church, which also includes the Bell, a 14th-century stone-built coaching inn. St Mary's church is an unpretentious building, where pride of place must go to the 17th-century pulpit. This exquisite piece of craftsmanship is carved with fruit-bearing trees in its main panels, and must have provided an interesting diversion for the congregation during many a dull sermon! In **TYTHERINGTON**

lies another unpretentious church building. St James, a single-cell chapel, has sat on a grassy knoll by a bend in the road since 1083. The information board outside the church states that it was endowed by the Empress Mathilda, mother of Henry II, in 1140.

GROVELY WOOD
An ancient forest that lies between the River Wylye to the north and east, and the River Nadder to the south. The best time to visit the wood is on 29th May, Oak Apple Day, when an ancient custom known as the *Grovely Forest Rights* is enacted. This annual ceremony is where the people of Great Wishford claim their right to collect 'all kinde of deade snappinge woode, boughes and stickes' from the local forest. Very early in the morning, the cry of 'Grovely, Grovely, Grovely and All Grovely' sounds forth, and the villagers proceed to the wood where an oak bough is cut. The bough is then decked in ribbons and carried ceremonially to Great Wishford church where it is hung from the tower.

Through the Longleat Estate

16 miles

The Longleat estate sits proudly on the Wiltshire-Somerset border, acres of rolling hills, deep woodland, landscaped parkland and secluded lakes, with the focus being on the Elizabethan mansion. To the north lies Cley Hill, a mecca for UFO spotters in the 1960s and 1970s, whilst to the south lies the Upper Wylye Valley, where one of Wiltshire's most noted chalk streams has its humble origins.

This circuit explores this quite delightful landscape, and the attractive villages that lie along the way. The countryside throughout is undulating, but do not worry about the occasional uphill stretches – the reward is always a far-ranging view across a delightfully secluded corner of the West Country. The highlight will undoubtedly be cycling along the main driveway in front of Longleat House, and feeling very much part of the landed gentry . . . if only for a few moments!

Map: OS Landranger 183 Yeovil and Frome (GR 854420).

Starting point: The Shearwater car park. Follow the A350 south from Warminster for 1 mile until, just past the Longbridge Deverill village sign, a right turn is signposted to Shearwater. Follow this turning for ¼ mile before turning left into Cley Street by the Bath Arms. The car park is on the left in ¾ mile.

Refreshments: There are pubs along the way at Horningsham, Maiden Bradley and Longbridge Deverill, as well as the Bargate Tearooms by Shearwater Lake at journey's end.

The route: Although most of the inclines are within the capabilities of a fairly average cyclist, there are one or two stretches where you may well need to walk your bicycle uphill. This is particularly the case for the ½ mile of the route south of Horningsham. The roads throughout are pretty quiet, with the exception of a short stretch of the A362 south of Cley Hill.

---

1. Return to the road alongside the car park, **turn R** and cycle along to the junction by the Bath Arms. **Turn L** and, in 600 yards, **L again** along a sharp left-turn signposted to Potters Hill. Follow this road for 1¾ miles to a T-junction, ignoring an early left turn to Potters Hill itself.

At the T-junction, at the end of Bucklers Wood, **turn R** down to the A362 and a busy roundabout. **Turn L**, and follow the main road downhill past Cley Hill for ½ mile, before **turning L** along the side turning signposted to the Longleat Safari Park.

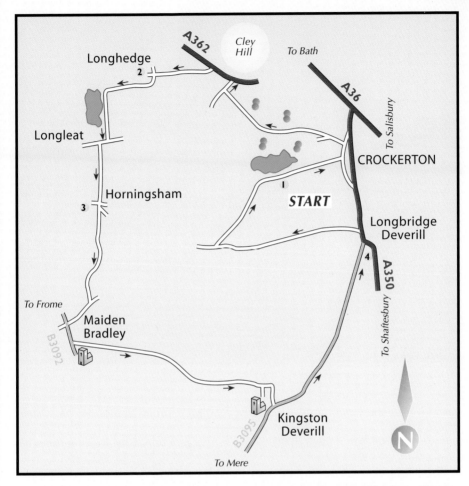

Follow this lane through the hamlet of Longhedge, keeping on the road as it **bears L** to cross a cattle grid and enter the Longleat Estate.

2. Follow the estate road uphill for 150 yards beyond this cattle grid, before **bearing R** to continue along the road as it borders the safari park. Keep on the road for ¾ mile to a point where it bears left to reach the pay booths for the safari park. Pass to **the R** of these pay booths – look out for the Wiltshire Cycleway sign – and through a gap in

the fence made especially for cyclists, and continue along the estate road still bordering the safari park.

Follow this road for ½ mile to a T-junction, **turn R** and head down to Longleat House and **then L** in front of the mansion to follow the long drive up to an arched entrance lodge. Beyond this lodge, follow the road on uphill to reach the crossroads in Horningsham by the Bath Arms Inn.

3. Follow the lane opposite signposted

79

Shearwater Lake at the start of the route

to Maiden Bradley and Mere. In 1½ miles, at the next junction, **turn R** and follow the next section of road for ½ mile to the B3092 in Maiden Bradley.

Turn L along the B3092 and, in 250 yards, **turn L** along the lane to Kingston Deverill, just before the church. Follow this lane for 3¼ miles to the B3095 in Kingston Deverill, the lane bearing right just past a bungalow called Lynchets to reach the 'B' road by the village church.

Turn L, and follow the B3095 through the Wylye Valley for 3 miles to the A350 in Longbridge Deverill.

4. Turn L, pass the George Inn and then take the **first L** signposted to Maiden Bradley. Follow this lane as it

climbs gently but steadily to reach a road junction in 2 miles.

At this junction, **turn R** along the road signposted to Warminster and Shaftesbury. Follow this lane for 1¾ miles back to the Shearwater car park.

● ● ● ● ● ● ● ● ● ● ● ● ● ● ● ● ● ● ●

SHEARWATER LAKE
The starting point for this route, Shearwater Lake covers an area of some 35 acres. The Duke of Bridgwater constructed it in the late 18th century, by damming a small stream that flowed through this delightful woodland valley. Rhododendrons grow over the water's edge along most of the shoreline, overshadowed by broad-leaved trees such as beech and oak that were planted over 100 years ago. The lake and surrounding

woodland attract a large variety of birds and other wildfowl, that include little grebes, grey heron, tufted duck, woodpeckers, pied wagtails and tawny owls.

CLEY HILL

Cley Hill, some 750 feet in height, is a distinctive chalk knoll that stands in splendid isolation amidst a generally flat agricultural landscape. Atop the hill are the remains of a Bronze Age hillfort within whose ramparts lie a pair of distinctive round barrows. In the late 1960s, Cley Hill was a mecca for UFO hunters, with many alleged sightings from its summit on clear summer evenings. Books with strange titles like *UFOs over Warminster* appeared on the market, and hotels in this nearby town

reported a boom in trade. The 'believers' explained these phenomena with reference to ley lines, several of which converge on Warminster, whilst cynics pointed out the army exercises on nearby Salisbury Plain that caused many lights in the night sky!

LONGLEAT HOUSE

The first stately home to open its doors to the public, way back in 1949. The family seat of the Marquess of Bath, Longleat is set in a vast parkland that includes some 5,000 acres of estate woodland. Sir John Thynne's house of 1550, built on the site of a 13th-century Augustinian priory, was largely destroyed by fire. The four-square building of 1567–79 features rectangular windows, mullioned and transomed, and each of

Cley Hill

The 16th-century Longleat House

the facades is similarly designed. In 1757, 'Capability' Brown cleared away the former gardens, created a formal garden and landscaped the area to give it the appearance that today's visitors enjoy.

He was also responsible for the stable block and the orangery. The Safari Park was set up in 1966, and its residents include giraffes and camels, monkeys and gorillas.

Glastonbury and Baltonsborough

20 miles

Glastonbury is widely acknowledged to be one of the most mystical and mysterious places in Britain. The Tor, with the ruinous tower of what was formerly St Michael's church, is an ever-present landmark in this part of Somerset. Its presence is felt at every turn on this route, providing a focus in what is otherwise a flat or gently undulating landscape.

South of Glastonbury lie a number of sleepy rural villages that include Butleigh and Baltonsborough, each with an interesting tale to tell from centuries past. The landscape may well be – to quote one local author – 'excessively horizontal', but it is never short of interest with expansive open views at every turn. With a complete lack of significant gradients, it is not difficult to see why this area has become popular cycling country.

Map: OS Landranger 182 Weston-super-Mare and Bridgwater (GR 501389).

Starting point: Silver Street car park, which lies behind the High Street in Glastonbury. To reach Silver Street, turn off the A361 by the Rural Life Museum in Glastonbury into Chilkwell Street. Silver Street is then the first turning on the left-hand side.

Refreshments: There are no shortages of pubs and hostelries on this route, with every village having a watering hole for thirsty cyclists. In Glastonbury itself, the choice of catering establishments is vast, with tea-rooms and cafes, restaurants and pubs at every turn.

The route: Apart from the inevitable traffic in Glastonbury itself, and the need to cross the A39 and the A361 along the way, this route follows generally flat and quiet lanes that cross the eastern fringes of the Somerset Levels. The terrain is so flat that the one or two gentle inclines around West Pennard and Butleigh come as something of a shock!

---

1. Cycle up Silver Street to join Chilkwell Street, **turn L** and then **next L** into Glastonbury's High Street. At the bottom of the High Street, by the Market Place and the Market Cross, **turn R** by the King William public house into the semi-pedestrianised Northload Street.

Follow this road for 600 yards to the Northload Bridge Roundabout, and head directly across to follow the B3151 Meare Road. In 200 yards, take the **R turn** signposted to Godney which shortly passes the local football ground.

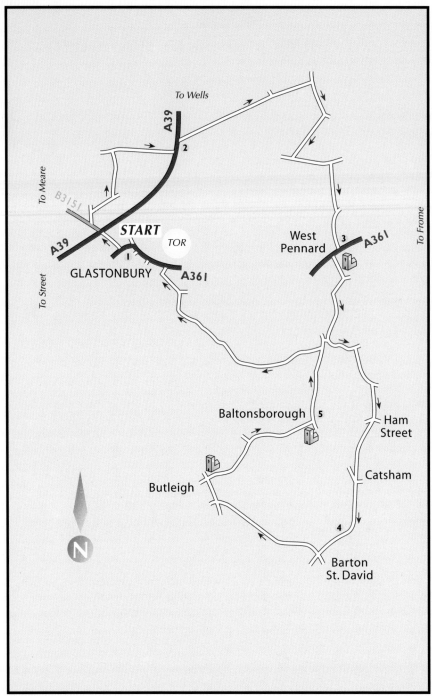

Baltonsborough

Just past the football ground, **turn R** by Sweet Acre Nursery. In ¼ mile, **turn L** and head across Common Moor. In ¾ mile, at the next junction, **turn R** and follow a lane for ¾ mile to reach the A39.

2. Cross the A39 to join the cyclepath opposite. Follow this path **to the L** for 250 yards before **turning R** along the lane signposted to Launcherley.

Follow this straight byway for 2¼ miles across Queen's Sedge Moor to a T-junction. **Turn R** and, ignoring one left turn along the way, follow this road for 1¼ miles to the next junction. **Keep L** alongside a drainage channel called simply Redlake.

In ¾ mile, by Redlake Farm, take the **R**

turn signposted to West Pennard and Glastonbury. Follow this lane for 1¼ miles to reach West Pennard and the A361.

3. Turn R along the A361, passing the Red Lion Inn, before taking the **first L** by Corner Garage signposted to West Bradley. Follow the West Bradley road for 1 mile to reach the National Trust's Court Barn.

Continue along this road for another ½ mile before **turning R** at a junction by a detached property on a road signposted to Baltonsborough (NB. ignore an earlier right turn to the same village). Pass Bridge Farm and, in ½ mile, **turn R** into the delightfully named Teapot Lane. In 600 yards, at a junction in Ham Street, **turn R** and then **immediately L** along the road to Barton St David.

In ¾ mile, at a junction in the hamlet of Catsham, keep ahead along the road signposted to Barton St David. Follow this lane, which shortly borders the River Brue and crosses Tootle Bridge before entering Barton St David.

4. Cycle through the village to a staggered crossroads by a telephone box. **Turn R** along Main Street, signposted to Butleigh. Having passed Barton Inn on the left, continue for 1 mile into Butleigh.

Cycle through the village to a crossroads by the Rose and Portcullis pub. **Turn R** – signposted to

Glastonbury and Street – and continue for ¼ mile to another crossroads. **Turn R** – signposted to Baltonsborough and West Pennard – and cycle along Butleigh's High Street passing the church, the post office and the school.

Immediately past the school, **turn L** along Baltonsborough Road. Continue for 1¼ miles to a crossroads in Baltonsborough by the Greyhound Inn.

5. **Turn L** – signposted to Glastonbury and West Pennard. In 1¼ miles, just past the Coxbridge village sign, **turn L** along an unmarked lane. Follow this quiet byway for 3¼ miles across Kennard Moor.

Keep on this lane as it eventually bears

The River Brue

right away from the River Brue in the general direction of Glastonbury Tor to reach a T-junction. **Turn L** and, in 600 yards, keep on the lane as it bears right by a play area to climb steeply uphill to reach the A361. **Turn L** to reach a roundabout by the Rural Life Museum in Glastonbury in just 300 yards. **Turn R** into Chilkwell Street, before taking the **first L** into Silver Street.

● ●

GLASTONBURY

Glastonbury is a place of legend. The Glastonbury Thorn that grows on Wearyall Hill and in the Abbey grounds allegedly sprouted from the staff of Joseph of Arimathea, visiting Britain after the Crucifixion; the waters of the Chalice Well flow red because Joseph is said to have deposited the Chalice Cup of the Last Supper beneath its waters . . . although the presence of local iron deposits may just be nearer the truth! The bodies of King Arthur and Queen Guinevere are said to repose in the Abbey grounds, with the site of the tomb still commemorated with a plaque, whilst the Tor was supposedly the entrance to the Underworld, the Kingdom of Annwn. Certainly, the town acts as a magnet to any number of travelling folk whose beards, beads and balding pates dominate the local high street!

BUTLEIGH

Perhaps the best known resident to figure in Butleigh's history was the Reverend Hood, whose three sons all achieved fame as sailors. When he was superseded in 1793, Nelson wrote: 'The Fleet must regret the loss of Lord Hood, the best officer, taken altogether, that England has to boast of: great in all situations which an Admiral can be placed in.' A rather lengthy epitaph by the poet Southey, dedicated to the Hoods, appears in Butleigh church. Visitors should not get too excited, however, with this poetic tribute having been described as 'a pedestrian muse if ever there was one'.

BALTONSBOROUGH

Baltonsborough was the birthplace of St Dunstan in the early years of the 10th century. As a young man, he won favour with King Athelstan, soothing the troubled brow of the sovereign with his musical abilities. Soon, however, he was to forsake the pleasures of the flesh by entering the strict regime of Glastonbury Abbey. Here he constructed a hermit's cell for himself that measured a mere 5 feet by 2½ feet! The devil ill-advisedly visited Dunstan on one occasion in an attempt to lure him away from his pious lifestyle, only to have his nose tweaked by a set of red-hot tongs . . . at least, that is the story portrayed on the banner in Baltonsborough church! By 940 AD, the zealous Dunstan had become Abbot of Glastonbury, whilst 19 years later he had risen to the venerable rank of Archbishop of Canterbury. Dunstan's birthplace was **HAM STREET**, the diminutive settlement a mile east of Baltonsborough that is passed along the way. A memorial of Doulting limestone has been erected in Ham Street to commemorate the local boy made good.

19

Glastonbury, Coxley and Godney

19 miles

To the west of the magical and mystical town of Glastonbury lie the Peat Moors, vast tracts of flat low-lying land, formerly primeval marsh, protected from flooding by a network of drainage ditches, pumping stations and sluices. This is an open landscape with barely a hedgerow in sight, crossed by a series of long, straight lanes and byways that make for perfect cycling. The route first heads north, towards Coxley and then the motte and bailey of Fenny Castle, before turning westward to Westhay Moor. Of interest on the return will be the site of a former lake village, now little more than a series of almost imperceptible mounds. If it is natural history rather than ancient history that is your interest, however, Westhay Moor will certainly not disappoint. A series of flooded peat workings, this is a wildfowl site of international importance.

Map: OS Landranger 182 Weston-super-Mare and Bridgwater (GR 494397).

Starting point: The car park by Glastonbury Football Ground. This is reached by taking the B3151 Meare turning off the Glastonbury bypass, before taking the first right turn signposted to Godney. The football ground is on the right-hand side of this lane.

Refreshments: The route passes the Riverside Restaurant in Coxley, as well as the Sheppey Inn at Godney, although a packed lunch enjoyed alongside the lakes and ponds on Westhay Moor is perhaps a better alternative. Back in Glastonbury, almost every conceivable taste in food and drink is catered for.

The route: Apart from having to cross the busy A39 running between Glastonbury and Wells on a couple of occasions, this route follows generally flat and quiet lanes in-and-around Somerset's peat moors. The terrain is so flat that the one or two insignificant hills around Coxley will come as a real shock! There is a 1¼ mile stretch of off-road cycling as the route follows an unmetalled track across Westhay Moor, where the occasional sharp piece of gravel will need to be avoided.

1. Leave the car park, **turn R** and then almost immediately **turn R again** by Sweet Acre Nursery. Follow the lane ahead for 1 mile to a T-junction, ignoring all side turns along the way, before **turning R** along Chasey's Drove to join the A39 in ½ mile.

Cross WITH CARE to join the cyclepath opposite, and follow this path **to the L**, crossing Hartlake Bridge before reaching a **R-turn** signposted to Launcherley.

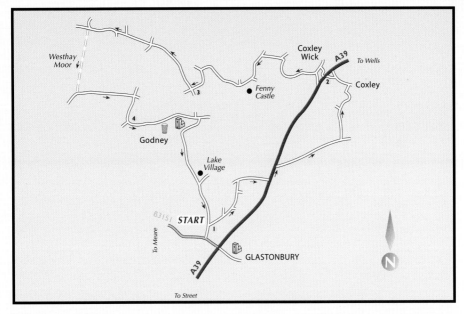

Follow this straight lane for 1½ miles to a **L-turn** marked by a stone carving bearing the legend 'Wells 3¾'. **Turn L** and follow this lane northwards for 1 mile to a T-junction on the edge of Coxley. **Turn L** into the village and, in 300 yards, **turn L** by The Old Post Office to follow a side turning down to the A39

2. Cross over into Mill Lane, passing the Riverside Restaurant, cross the River Sheppey and follow the lane as it winds its way up out of Coxley to a T-junction on the edge of neighbouring Coxley Wick.

Turn L and, in just 250 yards, **turn R** into Haymoor Lane opposite a small estate of houses called Orchard Leigh. Follow the lane downhill out of Coxley Wick for 1 mile to a junction on the edge of Hay Moor. **Turn L** and, in 600 yards, **L again** at a T-junction by Pine Tree Farm.

Follow this lane for 1¾ miles to a crossroads, with the lane passing Fenny

Castle as well as bordering the River Sheppey along the way. Ignore one left-turn and two right-turns on this section of the route, always keeping on the road signposted to Godney.

3. At the crossroads, take the **R turn** signposted to Panborough and Wedmore. In 1¼ miles, at an unsigned crossroads, keep ahead along North Chine Drove.

In another 1¼ miles, the route reaches another crossroads where the right turn carries a 'Weak Bridge' sign. At this point, **turn L** and follow Dagg's Lane Drove, an unmetalled track, for 1¼ miles across Westhay Moor, passing through the Westhay Moor Nature Reserve along the way.

At the southern end of the drove, by a parking area, **turn L** along Westhay Moor Drove. Follow this lane for 1¼ miles to a crossroads, and **turn R** along the lane signposted to Godney.

Peat workings on Westhay Moor

4. In ½ mile, keep on the lane as it bears left into Godney. Follow the lane through this scattered hamlet, passing the Sheppey Inn, for just under 1½ miles to reach a staggered crossroads. **Turn R** along the lane signposted to Glastonbury.

Follow this lane back towards Glastonbury, passing Godney church just outside of the village. Towards the end of the ride there are **two L turns** – the site of the Lake Village lies alongside the first turning, whilst the car park lies just beyond the second turning.

● ● ● ● ● ● ● ● ● ● ● ● ● ● ● ● ● ● ●

WESTHAY MOOR

The Moor was described in the Middle Ages as being 'wet and weely, miry and moorish'. This is rather a gloomy picture for a landscape that has more recently been described as 'wild country . . . fascinating and quite magical'. The second description is far closer to the truth! The damp, low-lying peat moor is criss-crossed by a network of drainage ditches, known locally as 'rhynes'. This watery environment provides a natural home for such diverse wildfowl as swans, herons and kingfishers, whilst flocks of peewits are a common sight in the surrounding fields. Part of the exhausted peat working has been purchased by the Somerset Trust for Nature Conservation and is being developed as Greater Westhay Reserve. Alder and willow have been planted, and extensive reed beds developed. The Reserve has attracted badgers and foxes, kestrels and coots, as well as large numbers of dragonfly.

THE GLASTONBURY LAKE VILLAGE

Now little more than a few diminutive bumps in the ground to the untrained eye, this has proven to be an exciting discovery for archaeologists. Here have been excavated Celtic lake dwellings, artificial islands made over two thousand year ago. These dwellings were built on artificial mounds made in shallow water near what was then the shore of a lake. Constructed of tree trunks, earth and stone, the islands were connected to the mainland by a raised causeway. The Tribunal, a small museum in Glastonbury's High Street, has displays that relate to the Lake Village, including a number of finds unearthed following excavations at the site. If all this talk of lakes and shorelines sounds somewhat confusing in a landscape of open countryside, it must be remembered that until the coming of sea-defences and drainage schemes, much of the Somerset Levels resembled either marshy bog or an open lake.

Along the way

Westhay, Meare and Mark

22 miles

The Somerset Levels, a vast area of damp lowland, is certainly one of the more unique habitats in the country. The landscape may be flat, but it is most definitely not dull or featureless. Formerly a waterlogged, low-lying marsh, extensive drainage has left the area with a dense network of rhynes, drainage ditches and watercourses. These in turn provide the perfect habitat for moisture-loving plants and wildfowl. You can discover more about this ancient historical landscape at the Peat Moors Visitor Centre, or find the perfect spot for a riverside picnic at Mark.

As well as the villages of Westhay, Meare, Burtle and Mark, this route passes through Westhay Moor and Shapwick Heath Nature Reserves. What were formerly peat workings have been planted with traditional wetland reeds and grasses, which now attract a rich variety of wildlife that includes many unusual species of dragonfly and butterfly. An added bonus is the complete absence of contour lines – perfect cycling country in fact!

Map: OS Landranger 182 Weston-super-Mare and Bridgwater (GR 456437).

Starting point: Westhay Moor Nature Reserve car park. Half a mile north of Westhay, on the B3151 road from Glastonbury to Wedmore, a minor road is signposted to Godney. The parking area lies 1¼ miles along this lane, just alongside a sharp right-hand bend.

Refreshments: Along the way, there are inns at Westhay, Ashcott Corner, Burtle and Mark. The 17th-century White Horse at Mark, with its spacious garden, is particularly recommended. This hostelry lies a good two-thirds of the way around the circuit, and is renowned for offering a wide choice of home-made food, well-kept beers and even decent coffee!

The route: The circuit does include a couple of off-road sections – a 2-mile track across Shapwick Heath and a similar track across Westhay Moor. The occasional large lump of sharp gravel should be obviously avoided, although the odds on a puncture are minimal.

1. Return to the road from the parking area, **turn R** and cycle the 1¼ miles to the B3151 Glastonbury road. **Turn L**, signposted to Westhay and Meare, and cycle the short distance to Westhay.

Cross the River Brue and, immediately past the Bird in Hand pub, **turn left** along a lane called Meareway. Follow this back lane for 1 mile through to the B3151 in Meare. **Turn L** and, in 300

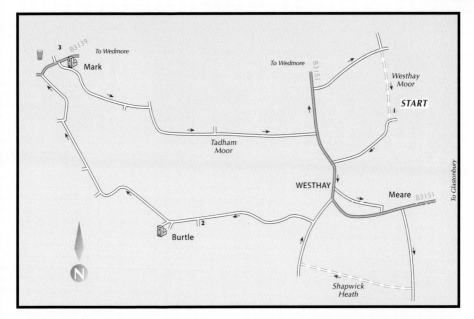

yards, **turn R** into Ashcott Road.

Follow this road south for 1¼ miles to the Railway Inn at Ashcott Corner, cross the South Drain and immediately **turn R** to enter the Shapwick Heath National Nature Reserve. Follow the unmetalled track across the reserve for 2 miles to join Shapwick Road.

Turn R, and cycle towards Westhay, passing the Peat Moors Visitors Centre along the way. In ¾ mile, on entering Westhay, **turn L** by New House Farm into Burtle Road. Follow this lane for 2 miles to the Burtle Inn, at Burtle.

2. Continue along the 'main' road through Burtle towards Mark and Wedmore. In 2 miles, keep on this road as it bears right to cross the River Brue.

In another 600 yards, having crossed a drainage channel, ignore the left-turn to Brent Knoll, keeping ahead on the road signposted to Mark. In ¾ mile, at

the next junction, **turn R** and follow the lane signposted to Glastonbury. Follow this lane for ¾ mile around to the B3139 in Mark.

Turn R, pass the White Horse Inn and carry on through the village. In 250 yards, **turn R** immediately past the Packhorse Inn to follow Little Moor Road.

3. Follow this lane for 2 miles to a junction, ignoring one right turn along the way by Summerleaze Farm.

Turn R, and follow the lane for 3 miles to reach the B3151.

Turn L and, in ¾ mile, at a staggered crossroads, **turn R** along the lane that runs across the northern edge of Westhay Moor.

In 1¼ miles, at a crossroads, **turn R** down Daggs Lane Drove and follow a rough, unmetalled track for 1¼ miles

The route through Tadham Moor

through Westhay Reserve back to the parking area.

● ●

SHAPWICK HEATH

Shapwick Heath contains remnants of the raised bogs that once ran to within a few miles of the Somerset coast. A wide range of vegetation types is to be found on the heath, from poor fen and bog myrtle pastures through to birch and alder. The most obvious land-use, however, is peat extraction, with vast tracts of the heath looking for all intents and purposes like areas of open cast mining. The area is perhaps best known for its rich butterfly and dragonfly population, whilst it is not unknown for roe deer to be seen in the local thickets.

MARK

Situated on a causeway above what was formerly a flooded marsh area, the name 'Mark' literally means 'boundary' and is based upon the fact that the village stood on the edge of the mother parish of Wedmore. There is an imposing church in the village, whilst the banks of the Mark Yeo make a perfect resting place should you prefer a picnic rather than a visit to the nearby White Horse Inn.

WESTHAY

Westhay is a small village consisting largely of scattered farms. One of the local farmers, Mr Ray Sweet, was clearing the ditches on his land in 1970 when he stumbled across pieces of waterlogged timber and a flint arrowhead. Sensing a valuable find, expert archaeological advice was summoned and an ancient

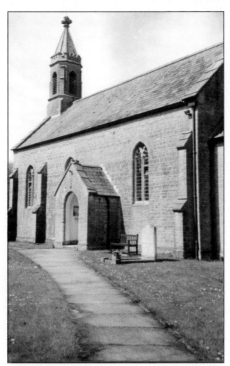
Burtle church

trackway was discovered. Subsequently named the Sweet Track, this routeway which dates from 4000 BC is believed to be the world's oldest footpath. Basically, what Ray Sweet had discovered was the remains of a gangway constructed of wooden poles, which enabled ancient fishermen and hunters to make their way across what was then a waterlogged landscape. The Willows Garden Centre, which is passed along the way, houses the Peat Moors Visitors Centre. As well as displays relating to the local peat industry, a mock-up section of the Sweet Way can be seen.

ROUTE GRADINGS

These subjective rankings are based upon such factors as the severity of gradients, traffic volumes, off-road cycling and mileage.

EASY CIRCUITS

1. Thornbury, Berkeley and Shepperdine
9. Castle Combe and Foxley
10. Through the Vale of Pewsey
19. Glastonbury, Coxley and Godney
20. Westhay, Meare and Mark

MODERATE CIRCUITS

2. Berkeley, Slimbridge and Sharpness
3. South Cerney, Kemble and the Cotswold Water Park
4. East of Malmesbury
5. Iron Acton, Wickwar and the Vale of Sodbury
6. Chipping Sodbury, Hawkesbury Upton and Hillesley
7. Badminton and Easton Grey
11. Through the Vale of Steeple Ashton
12. Holt, Lacock and Broughton Gifford
13. Bradford-on-Avon
18. Glastonbury and Baltonsborough

ADVENTUROUS CIRCUITS

8. Marshfield, Nettleton and Castle Combe
14. Norton St Philip, Beckington and Mells
15. Twerton, Compton Dando and Stanton Prior
16. Heytesbury, Grovely Wood and the Wylye Valley
17. Through the Longleat Estate